Hypnosis Therapy- Extreme Weight Loss, Deep Sleep & Anxiety (2 in 1):

Guided Meditations & Positive Affirmations For Rapid Fat Burn, Insomnia, Emotional Eating & Overthinking

Gastric Band & Deep Sleep Hypnosis:

Positive Affirmations & Guided Meditations For Rapid Weight Loss, Self-Love & Extreme Fat Burn+ Overcoming Insomnia, Body Anxiety & Overthinking

© Copyright 2021 - All rights reserved.

The content contained within this book may not be reproduced, duplicated or transmitted without direct written permission from the author or the publisher.

Under no circumstances will any blame or legal responsibility be held against the publisher, or author, for any damages, reparation, or monetary loss due to the information contained within this book; either directly or indirectly.

Legal Notice:
This book is copyright protected. This book is only for personal use. You cannot amend, distribute, sell, use, quote or paraphrase any part, or the content within this book, without the consent of the author or publisher.

Disclaimer Notice:
Please note the information contained within this document is for educational and entertainment purposes only. All effort has been executed to present accurate, up to date, and reliable, complete information. No warranties of any kind are declared or implied. Readers acknowledge that the author is not engaging in the rendering of legal, financial, medical or professional advice.

In this 10-hour series, we explore weight loss and deep sleep, naturally, through guided hypnosis, meditation and affirmations.

This audiobook will include a series of hypnotherapy sessions, guided meditations and affirmations, that will transform the hearts and minds of listeners who are desperately seeking ways to lose weight and combat insomnia.

All sessions are original content, written by a qualified Hypnotherapist with extensive experience in helping people achieve their personal life goals naturally.

The Sessions

The sessions will unfold as follows:

Session 1: Hypnosis Script - Deep Sleep...9

Session 2: Hypnosis Script - Body Anxiety & Overthinking............................. 17

Session 3: Hypnosis Script – Fat Burn & Exercise 24

Session 4: Hypnosis Script – Self-love & Integration 31

Session 5: Guided Meditation - Overcoming Insomnia 40

Session 6: Guided Meditation - Self Love & Weight Loss 47

Session 7: Guided Meditation - Deep Sleep For Rapid Weight Loss 56

Session 5: Affirmations - Overcoming Insomnia 65

Session 6: Affirmations - Extreme fat burn 68

Session 7: Affirmations - Overcoming Body Anxiety 71

Conclusion 74

Introduction:

About this Audiobook.

Hello and welcome to Weight Loss and Deep Sleep a 10-hr Audiobook, brought to you by _____ This powerful 10-hour series will provide you with powerful hypnosis to induce a natural and deep sleep every night and to achieve your ideal weight by working on self-image, exercise and fat burning naturally for rapid transformation!

Weight Loss and Deep Sleep is a series of powerful hypnosis audios, and transformational guided meditations, designed to unleash your mental capacity to drop the pounds, shed the fat fast and sleep well while doing it! There are also three bonus affirmation audios created especially for you to listen to on a daily basis to accelerate your weight loss journey!

Each session has been made using powerful hypnotherapeutic techniques to work on the limiting beliefs, resistances, lack of exercise and remove the blocks you hold to weight loss and overcoming insomnia easily.

Who this audiobook is suitable for

This audiobook is open for all who wish to lose weight, attain their weight goals and have trouble sleeping.

What results you can expect

This audiobook is very powerful and can entirely change one's beliefs, actions, resistances, and behaviours linked to weight loss and deep sleep. Repetition is required in order to gain the full benefits from this powerful process.

How to use this content.

It is recommended that the listener is in a place where they can have at least 30-60 minutes of time to themselves depending on which session is being listened to.

Simply find a place to either sit down or lie down comfortably. It is also recommended that the listener uses earphones or headphones for maximum effect, however they are not entirely necessary.

Session 1. Weight Loss and Deep Sleep: Hypnosis Session - Deep Sleep

Overview:
A 60-min Hypnosis session.

This session will focus on direct suggestions to help the listener fall asleep whenever they go to bed. Including powerful induction deepeners, metaphors, direct suggestions and ego-strengthening.

Session 2. Weight Loss and Deep Sleep: Hypnosis Session - Body Anxiety & Overthinking

Overview:
A 60-min Hypnosis session.

This session will focus on overcoming body anxiety and putting an end to overthinking. The session includes powerful induction, deepeners and the use of a powerful metaphor to overcome body anxiety and overthinking along with direct suggestion and ego-strengthening.

Session 3. Weight Loss and Deep Sleep: Hypnosis Session - Fat Burn & Exercise

Overview:
A 60-min Hypnosis session.

This session will focus on direct suggestions for fat burning and motivation for exercising daily. Includes induction, deepeners, a collection of suggestions to focus on exercise and a metaphor for increased fat burning and ego-strengthening.

Session 4. Weight Loss and Deep Sleep: Hypnosis Session - Self Love and Integration

Overview:
A 60-min Hypnosis session.

This session will focus on reconnecting the listener to self-love by using parts dissociation therapy and sealing off the sessions with self-integration work. Includes induction, deepeners, parts therapy for self-love and self-integration therapy for maintenance and ego-strengthening.

Session 5. Weight Loss and Deep Sleep: Guided Meditation - Overcoming insomnia

Overview:
A 30-min Guided meditation

This guided meditation will focus on addressing our anxieties so that we can release our mind of stress and worries, allowing us to fall into a state of relaxation and to enjoy a deep, uninterrupted sleep.

Session 6. Weight Loss and Deep Sleep: Guided Meditation - Self Love & Weight Loss

Overview:
A 30-min Guided meditation

This guided meditation will focus on embracing self love and acceptance of ourselves. By encouraging self love, we allow ourselves to progress on our weightloss journey, no longer hindered by a belief that we do not deserve a healthy and happy future.

Session 7. Weight Loss and Deep Sleep: Guided Meditation - Deep Sleep for Rapid Weight Loss

Overview:
A 60-min Guided meditation
This meditation will take the listener on a visual journey, guiding them into a state of intense relaxation that will result in a deep sleep and encourage rapid weight loss.

Session 8. Weight Loss and Deep Sleep: Affirmations - Overcoming Insomnia and Weight Loss

Overview:
A 30-min Subliminal affirmation session

This session will include a series of powerful present moment affirmations that will reinforce the reprogramming of the previous hypnotic sessions. These affirmations will focus on the topic of overcoming insomnia.

Session 9. Weight Loss and Deep Sleep: Affirmations - Extreme Fat Burn

Overview:
A 30-min Subliminal affirmation session

This session will include a series of powerful present moment affirmations that will reinforce the reprogramming of the previous hypnotic sessions. These affirmations will focus on the topics of extreme fat burn.

Session 10. Weight Loss and Deep Sleep: Affirmations - Body Anxiety

Overview:
A 30-min Subliminal affirmation session.

This session will include a series of powerful present moment affirmations that will reinforce the reprogramming of the previous hypnotic sessions. These affirmations will focus on the topics of body anxiety.

Session 1: Hypnosis Script - Deep Sleep

Overview: This session will focus on direct suggestions to help the listener fall asleep whenever they go to bed.

Time: 60-minutes

[Reader Notes]

- The rhythm and pace are important therefore please read the following script at a steady pace, ensuring to take your time to guide the listener with your voice.
- Allow long comfortable pauses in between passages that you are happy with, and follow the key set out below to allow longer pauses.
- Embedded commands: Embedded commands will be written in **bold**, the reader must read the bold phrases at a slightly faster pace than the rest of the script. Eg: "See how easy it is to **Just Relax** Nowww", See how easy it is should be ready normally while "just relax" should be read slightly faster returning back to the normal pace when reading "Nowww".
- Nowww: The word "Nowww" should be emphasized and said on an out-breath as if sighing.

[Pause Key]

… Very short pause: Reader pauses for 2 seconds

/ Short pause: Reader pauses for 10 seconds

// Medium pause: Reader pauses for 20 seconds

/// Long pause: Reader pauses for 30 seconds

[Script Begins]

Welcome to the first session in the Weight-loss and Deep Sleep audiobook! A Hypnosis/Guided Meditation series.

This powerful hypnosis audio will focus on helping you get a good night's rest by working directly with your unconscious mind to induce deep sleep.

Begin by finding a comfortable place where you can be alone for just a little while...

You can either sit down comfortably or lie down, please make sure your arms are by your sides and are uncrossed throughout the session.

Now you are in position, simply allow your eyes to close and imagine a wave of relaxation **travelling down** all the way **down**... from the top of your head to the tips of your toes... as you bring your awareness to your breath simply allow yourself to breathe in healing soothing light that is cleansing your entire body from the top of your head to the tips of your toes... and as you breathe out... allow dirty diseased energy to be exhaled out of your body through your breath... guiding yourself 2 times deeper and deeper... that's right...

And you may hear sounds around you... any sounds inside the room and perhaps you can hear sounds outside the room... how soon will it be before all these sounds will **fade away** into the background... as you disregard these sounds... and allow these sounds to guide you deeper and deeper...

Allowing a wave of descending bliss to take over you... relaxing you more and more... In a moment you will hear me say the word... Nowww and whenever you hear me say the word... Nowww... all the unnecessary nervous tension in your body can... **just relax**... and you can continue to **sink 5 times deeper**... into that wonderful state of peace... that wonderful relaxing state of openness...

So... Nowww... **let go**... drift... float... and descend... deeper and deeper with every word that I say...

And... Nowww... I would like you to imagine a brilliant ball of light floating above your head... this brilliant ball of light has the ability to remove all tension out of anything it comes into contact with... in a moment when I say the word **descend**... I would like you to feel and imagine this ball moving down slowly from the top of your head **down,** relaxing each part of your body that it comes in contact with...

So ready... **descend**... feel and imagine this ball **going down** onto the top of your head... down to your face... relaxing all the muscles in your head and face... and Nowww... allow the ball to **descend further down**... down to your neck and shoulders... allow all the muscles in your neck and shoulders to **just relax**... that's right... Now allowing the ball to expand and **descend**

down encompassing your arms and upper chest…allow all the muscles in your arms and chest to simply **relax**… let them become loose and limp…

And… Nowww… allowing the ball to **descend further down** encompassing your abdomen, elbows, hands, and fingers… allow them to relax… **relax completely**…
You're doing really well… allow the ball to **descend down**… into your hips and thighs… allow the muscles of your hips and thighs to simply relax…let them go… loose and limp relaxed…

And Nowww… the ball can **descend** encompassing your knees, shins, and calves… allow these muscles to **relax completely**…

Finally… Nowww… allow the ball to **descend** down to your ankles and feet… allow the ball to relax the muscles of your ankles and feet…Nowww… Very good…
Allow the ball to now **descend down**…**down** through the ground and **all the way down**… into the earth… allowing the earth to reabsorb and reuse this energy for something better… Leaving you with a sense of peace… a sense of calm soothing relaxation … that's right…

And soon… you will hear me count down from 10 to 1… and with each number I count down from 10 to 1 …with each descending number you are going 10 times deeper and deeper… so ready…10… Going deeper and deeper…9… Feeling better and better… 8 … The deeper you go the better you feel… 7… The better you feel the deeper you go… 6… drifting ever more deeper still… and 5… and 4… letting go… 3 … feeling free… 2… you are almost there… and…1…

Remain deeply relaxed… staying deeply relaxed… I would like to speak with your unconscious mind about a matter of importance… important to you…
And…Nowww… I would like your unconscious mind, the part of you that has the answer to all problems… the part of you that has access to all parts of you… to go searching within yourself for the part of you that is preventing sleep.

And I would like your unconscious mind to bring this part out and float it above your left hand…

/

Notice what this part may look like… perhaps it has a sound… or perhaps it has a feeling… or maybe even all three… however **this part manifests to you** now… become aware of it for a moment…

//

We shall refer to this part as the problem part… I would like you to now ask this problem part for insight as to what it is really doing for you…why is it really here… take a moment to interact with this part in this way Nowww…

//

Nowww… let this part know… that whatever this part needs to **easily sleep all night** now… there is another part of you that has exactly what this part needs to **easily sleep all night** now…

//

Let this part know that you will now go searching for the part of you that has exactly what that part needs to **easily sleep all night**…

//

So Nowww… I would like you to thank the problem part and leave it be for the moment above your left hand…

And I would now like your unconscious mind to go searching within yourself for the part of you that has the solution… the part of you that has exactly what this part needs to **easily sleep all night** now…

And I would like your unconscious mind to bring this part out and float it above your right hand…

/

Notice what this part may look like… perhaps it has a sound… or perhaps it has a feeling… or maybe even all three… however **this part manifests to you** now… become aware of it for a moment…

//

We shall refer to this part as the solution part… I would like you to now ask this solution part for insight as to what it will do for you… take a moment to interact with this part in this way Nowww…

//

I would like you to thank this part for its insight… and now I will begin to count up from 1 to 5 and with each number I count up, this solution part will become stronger…and stronger… and on the count of 5, this solution part will be 10 times stronger than the problem part…

So ready… 1… increasing the strength of the solution part… 2 more and more… 3 the solution part is already much stronger than the problem part… 4… and … 5 the solution part is now 10 times stronger than the problem part…

Become aware of any changes that may have occurred during the strengthening process of the solution part…

//

And Now… in whatever way is appropriate for you… put the two parts together… merge the problem part with the solution part…

Since the solution is 10 times stronger than the problem… the solution part engulfs the problem part giving it exactly what it needs to **easily sleep all night** now…

As these two parts now merge… it forms a unified part which is now floating in the centre in between your hands…

/

Notice what this unified part may look like… perhaps it has a sound… or perhaps it has a feeling… or maybe even all three… however **this part manifests to you** now… become aware of it for a moment…

//

I would like you to thank this part for whatever it will do for you…

//

And Nowww… I would like you to reintegrate this part back within yourself… I will give you a moment of time to carry this out…

//

Very good... Nowww... I would like you to go back in time now to a memory or time when you were able to sleep very easily and deeply... perhaps this was sooner than you think... perhaps this was later... perhaps it was early childhood... whenever this was ... remember what this was like... and if you cannot find a memory... that is ok... simply imagine what it would be like to have a very restful night's sleep easily and deeply Nowww... I will give you a moment to do this...

///

Now that you are experiencing this memory... or creating it in your mind... see what you would see... perhaps being aware of what it would be like to wake up in the morning after a very sound... pleasant... restful... uninterrupted and deep sleep...

Your unconscious mind always knows how to induce deep sleep in you... you already know how to **fall asleep easily**... how to **sleep all night**... how to **sleep without interruption**... you have done this before very easily as a baby... now it is time to reconnect to something so easy... you've simply forgotten how easy it was... now it is time to remember... and you are now open and ready to remember... remember how to **fall asleep easily**... remember how to **sleep all night**... and how to **sleep without interruption**... that's right...

Every day you will begin to feel more relaxed... very calm... and relaxed... with a greater sense of self control... each and every day... as bedtime approaches... you will feel more and more pleasantly tired... each day... you will go to bed at the same time... each night at the same time... and as soon as you put your head on the pillow... you will begin to instantly relax...Nowww... exactly as you do...as you listen to this recording... your mind will become calm and relaxed... your whole body relaxes too... and as it does so more and more... you will begin to feel a pleasant feeling of heaviness in your body... as if... it is beginning to feel like lead... heavy as lead... as if it is very comfortably sinking down... deeper and deeper... into the mattress... and as it does so.. you will feel drowsier and drowsier... more and more drowsy... and presently... you may even find... that you try to stay awake... and the harder you try to stay awake... the drowsier you become and you will feel drowsier and drowsier... your eyes will close... and you will fall into a natural... healthy sleep which will last throughout the night... until your usual time for getting up in the morning... if for any reason you should wake up in the night... you will simply fix your gaze on the ceiling... and as you do so your eyelids... will feel so heavy and tired... heavy and tired... wanting to close... more and more... and a pleasant feeling of relaxation and drowsiness will once again flow through you... and you may find that you try to stay awake... and the harder you try to stay awake the drowsier you become and you will feel drowsier and drowsier and then… within a very short time your eyes will close… and you will fall into a natural sleep again… which will last until your usual time for getting up in the morning… that's right allow your unconscious mind to receive these suggestions and communicate this to all parts of you…

Your unconscious mind always knows how to induce deep sleep in you… you already know how to **fall asleep easily**… how to **sleep all night**… how to **sleep without interruption**… you have done this before very easily as a baby… now it is time to reconnect to something so easy… you've simply forgotten how easy it was… now it is time to remember… and you are now open and ready to remember… remember how to **fall asleep easily**… remember how to **sleep all night**… and how to **sleep without interruption**… that's right…

As the days go by… these suggestions will begin to take effect within you… and begin to rebalance the sleep rhythm in your body and mind… putting them in sync… allowing your mind and body to fall asleep simultaneously… as soon as your head touches the pillow every night… if your mind is very active in bed… as soon as you lie down in bed… your mind will begin to relax… as each thought floats away …flows away like a boat in the sea… fading away… allowing your mind to relax… and Nowww there would be absolutely nothing for you to do right now… because regardless of what position you are lying down in… your body naturally adjusts itself to a comfortable position where your body can remain… allowing your mind and body both to **drift away …drift away into a deep and healthy slumber**… and a sound… pleasant sleep… with no interruptions… a refreshing… healing… rejuvenating and healthy sleep… until your usual time for getting up in the morning…

Sleep easily… and sleep well… as you fall asleep pleasantly…so you will begin to have pleasant dreams… empowering dreams… that will aid you in sleep… that will aid you in the tasks of the next day and that will empower you to achieve your goals…

/

And I will give you just a moment of time which is all the time you need to just relax… and this will also assist all my suggestions to **sink deep** into your unconscious mind…

///

And… Nowww…I would like to thank your unconscious mind for its cooperation… and before I awaken you… I want you to know that… as each day goes by you are going to become a little more mentally calm… a little more clear in your mind… each and every day… which means that you will see things more clearly… think more clearly… so that no-one and nothing will ever be able to affect you or upset you in quite the same way.. your mind becomes clearer and clearer... crystal clear... allowing you to feel physically calm and relaxed too... not only in your body but you will also feel more emotionally calm and more relaxed about yourself... and about the world around you...

And you can enjoy these feelings of wellbeing each and every day no matter what you're doing, where you are or who you're with and you will find that you are going to feel fitter and stronger in every way... feeling more energetic... feeling more alert... enjoying a greater and greater sense of positive energy.... Feeling motivated and encouraged, positive and optimistic... each and every day...
You are safe... in the knowledge that your unconscious mind is always looking out for you...

As every day you are going to experience a greater feeling of well-being, mental as well as physical well-being... a greater feeling of safety and security too than you have felt in a long ...long time... allowing you to live your life in a way that is so much more satisfying...satisfying for you...

/

And... Nowww... I will begin to count up from 1 to 10 and with each number, I count up you will become 10 percent more awake, by the count of 8 your eyes will open, and by the count of 10 you will be wide awake and fully alert... and all natural and normal sensations will return to your limbs... and you will wake up feeling, rested, rejuvenated, relaxed, happy, and wonderful, ready for the rest of the day... ready to achieve your ideal weight and your dream body...

So...1...2...3 Drifting towards wakefulness...4...5...6 waking up more and more...7...8...open your eyes... 9... and 10... Wide awake, wide awake...fully wide awake...

Thank you for listening to this powerful hypnosis audio, please remember that the results will continue to increase long after the session has finished. The results get profoundly deeper each time you listen to this recording.

Session 2: Hypnosis Script - Body Anxiety & Overthinking

Overview: This session will focus on overcoming body anxiety and putting an end to overthinking.

Time: 60-minutes

[Reader Notes]

- The rhythm and pace are important therefore please read the following script at a steady pace, ensuring to take your time to guide the listener with your voice.
- Allow long comfortable pauses in between passages that you are happy with, and follow the key set out below to allow longer pauses.
- Embedded commands: Embedded commands will be written in bold, the reader must read the bold phrases at a slightly faster pace than the rest of the script. Eg: "See how easy it is to **Just Relax** Nowww", See how easy it is should be ready normally while "just relax" should be read slightly faster returning back to the normal pace when reading "Nowww".
- Nowww: The word "Nowww" should be emphasized and said on an out-breath as if sighing.

[Pause Key]

… Very short pause: Reader pauses for 2 seconds

/ Short pause: Reader pauses for 10 seconds

// Medium pause: Reader pauses for 20 seconds

/// Long pause: Reader pauses for 30 seconds

_____

[Script Begins]

Welcome to the second session in the Weight-loss and Deep Sleep audiobook! A Hypnosis/Guided Meditation series.

This powerful hypnosis audio will focus on overcoming body anxiety and putting an end to patterns of overthinking.

Begin by finding a comfortable place where you can be alone for just a little while…
You can either sit down comfortably or lie down, please make sure your arms are by your sides and are uncrossed throughout the session.

Now you are in position, find a spot in front of you in the distance and simply gaze at this spot… and as you gaze at this spot notice as you breathe, each breath is relaxing you more and more…

Noticing that as you now stare at this spot your eyelids feel heavy and the more you stare the heavier your eyelids are becoming… heavier and heavier. …You may notice that you begin to blink more and more with each breath in… and each breath out… and I wonder how soon it will be before your eyes will close?… That's right just let your eyes close… let them close as you now bring your attention to your breath… And as you take a deep relaxing breath in through your nose… notice yourself going 3 times deeper with that breath out. That's right. Let go.

You may notice sounds around you, perhaps any sounds inside the room, or perhaps if you listen carefully you may hear sounds outside the room. All these sounds are unimportant, in fact in a strange and contradictory manner all these sounds will guide you deeper and deeper, making you feel better and better as the only sound of importance right now is the sound of my words and you can allow my words to pour relaxation throughout your mind… throughout your body… and throughout your awareness… that's right you're doing really well…

And… Nowww… I would like you to imagine that you are standing on a long empty road… notice what you may see… perhaps all the different shapes and shades of colours… noticing what time of day it is… becoming aware of the temperature of the air as it touches your skin… perhaps noticing the sounds around you… and as you breathe in… breathing in all those fragrances…

Now in a moment, I would like you to begin walking down this road… the road to change the way you see yourself… and how you think others perceive you… and how you perceive your body…

As you walk down this road... I will begin to count down from 10 to 1 and with each descending number from 10 and 1 ... each descending number will guide you 10 times deeper into that wonderful hypnotic state of relaxation... that in any event will become deeper and deeper as we go on... so... get ready...

Start walking down this road... the road to change... Nowww...10... Going deeper and deeper...9... Feeling better and better...with each step you take down this road... 8 ... The deeper you go the better you feel... 7... The better you feel the deeper you go... with each step you walk down this road 6... drifting ever more deeper still... and 5... feeling a sense of safety and security and 4... feeling a sense of optimism taking over you and you become open to letting go... 3 ... feeling free... 2... you are almost there... and...1... well done...

I would like you to know that every time I say the word deep... allow yourself to go 10 times deeper and deeper into that deep state of relaxation more and more...

And just know that the deeper you go the better you will feel and the better you will feel the deeper you will go... that's it...

Whenever I say the word fall, allow yourself to go 30 times deeper... so simply fall deep into that deep state of relaxation as you fall Nowww deep... deeper and deeper letting go... into that state of peace... into that state of calm soothing relaxation... pouring relaxation throughout your mind... throughout your body... and throughout your awareness... as you... fall deep Nowww...

And Nowww... as you reach the end of this road you see a grassy hill...and hear the sound of flowing water... as you follow the sound of the flowing water you see a grassy staircase leading down to a very magical looking riverbank...

The staircase contains 10 steps going down... approach this staircase and in a moment I will begin to countdown from 10 to 1 and with each descending number from 10 and 1 ... each descending number will guide you 20 times deeper into that wonderful hypnotic state of relaxation... that in any event will become even deeper and deeper as we go on... as you let go now...

Start walking down these stairs... these stairs leading down to the magical riverbank of change... Nowww...10... Going deeper and deeper...9... Feeling better and better...with each step you take down these stairs... 8 ... The deeper you go the better you feel... 7... The better you feel the deeper you go... with each step you walk down these stairs... 6... drifting ever more deeper still... moving closer and closer to the riverbank and 5... feeling a sense of safety and security and 4... feeling a sense of optimism taking over you and you become open to change and transformation... 3 ... feeling free... 2... you are almost there... and...1... you are doing really well...

Notice that you now stand before a very magical looking riverbank... the riverbank of change... the water of this very special riverbank has the ability to remove any worries... beliefs... labels... and anxieties related to how you feel about yourself... and how you feel about your body... the purifying water can remove all those worries about how you think other people may perceive you... notice that the water is clean and clear... smooth flowing.. beautiful... not a single rough edge or rock...

Notice what you may see here by this river bank... perhaps all the different shapes and shades of colours... perhaps any vegetation... becoming aware of the temperature of the air as it touches your skin... perhaps noticing the sounds around you... and as you breathe in... breathing in all those fragrances... around this riverbank... make this experience vivid and real for you...

Now move closer up to the water... and take a look at your reflection... in the water... and as you look at your reflection... begin to notice that all your insecurities are beginning to manifest itself in the reflection... all those worries... anxieties about yourself... about your body... and now notice that as you put your hands into the water... the magical river begins to pull out from you... ever so gently and pleasantly all those insecurities... being pulled out of you... all those worries.. all those anxieties about the way you look... about the way your body looks... and all those negative beliefs and labels about how other people perceive you... allow the river to pull them out and... watch them flow down the river... away from you... all your worries... anxieties... and negative beliefs about your appearance now... flowing away from you...in the river... the magical water... purifying them... allow this to take place for a moment now...

//

Nowww... that is done... imagine that all that is left of the insecurities... even those that may be too subtle for you to be aware of... your unconscious mind knows what they are.. simply allow these insecurities to drip down and out of your hands into the water... with each number I count down from 5 to 1... allow the last few insecurities that are left to trickle down your arms and right out of your palms and fingertips into the magical riverbank to flow right away from you Nowww... 5... feel those insecurities being accumulated and being pushed down from your shoulders... 4 ... you can let go of that heavy load now.... That you can feel lighter... allow it to flow down your arms...3... insecurities flowing down your elbows... 2... collecting in your palms ... the last few insecurities collecting in your palms... and... 1... allow them to drip right off your palms and into the water... flowing away from you... flick your hands into the water removing the last little drops... you are now... free... free from those burdens...

And Nowww... that all your worries... all your anxieties... and negative beliefs about your appearance and your body have now been pulled gently out of you and floated far away from you down the river...

Notice that there is a bridge nearby... that takes you to the other side of the river, approach this bridge and crossover to the other side... and notice that as you cross this bridge over the river... you are beginning to feel more and more optimistic about yourself... and when you cross to the other side... you notice there is a lake... this lake is still... it is so clear and steady... you can see the sky reflected off the surface of the still water... this water is like your mind... your thoughts... there are no ripples in the water... as you have been cleansed of all your anxieties and worries related to your body and how you and other people perceive your body...

Your mind can be crystal clear like this water... allow yourself to feel more and more confident about yourself... about the world around you and how other people perceive you... beauty... confidence and calmness lies within you... and you can begin to tap into it now... with each passing moment...

Similar to the riverbank this still water is also magical... a sip from this lake can produce a sense of confidence within yourself... connecting you to the eternal beauty that lies within you...

So... take a sip of the water from this still lake...and feel confidence flow through you... confidence about who you are... confidence about your body... confidence that you can achieve all your goals... you begin to feel more and more beautiful... and you know that when you feel beautiful inside... the world outside responds accordingly... so you know now consciously that as you tap into your inner confidence and inner beauty the world around you will see the confidence and beauty that you are ... that can flow out through you...

And soon I will begin to count up from 1 to 10 and with each number I count up these feelings of confidence and beauty will begin to increase more and more and on the count of 10, these feelings of confidence and beauty will be 10 times stronger... 10 times stronger than it has ever been before...

So ready... 1... feel those feelings of confidence increase more and more... with each number I count up... 2... beauty... inner beauty increases more and more... feel beautiful... 3... these feelings of confidence and beauty are now 3 times stronger... becoming stronger and stronger... 4 filling you from the top of your head to the tips of your toes Nowww... 5 beginning to smile as you tap into your inner beauty and confidence... 6... rushing through you... feel the optimism... feel the glow... emanating through you... 7... these feelings becoming 7 times stronger than they have ever been before... 8 becoming excited... very excited to go out there and allow your confidence and inner beauty to shine forth and illuminate your life... 9... feel it growing more and more throughout your mind... throughout your body... and throughout your awareness... that's right... and... 10... feelings of confidence and beauty now 10 times stronger... 10 times stronger than it has ever been before... feel yourself light up... like the sun shining anew... lighting up the path to inner change and inner transformation...

And I will give you just a moment of time which is all the time you need to just relax... and this will also assist all my suggestions to sink deep into your unconscious mind...

///

And... Nowww...I would like to thank your unconscious mind for its cooperation... and before I awaken you... I want you to know that... as each day goes by you are going to become a little more mentally calm... a little more clear in your mind... each and every day... which means that you will see things more clearly... think more clearly... so that no-one and nothing will ever be able to affect you or upset you in quite the same way.. your mind becomes clearer and clearer... crystal clear... allowing you to feel physically calm and relaxed too... not only in your body but you will also feel more emotionally calm and more relaxed about yourself... and about the world around you...

Every day...you will feel a positive sense of strength... your mind clearer and calmer... tranquil... serene and focused and as the days...weeks ...and months go by and you feel ever more calm and relaxed in your mind and body...you will find that you think more clearly... concentrate more effectively... giving your whole undivided attention to whatever you are doing... and consequently, you will be able to see things in their truest perspective... and you become emotionally calmer... every day you remain more and more relaxed physically, emotionally, and mentally...coping appropriately with each and every situation you handle in your daily life...

And you can enjoy these feelings of wellbeing each and every day no matter what you're doing, where you are or who you're with and you will find that you are going to feel fitter and stronger in every way... feeling more energetic... feeling more alert... enjoying a greater and greater sense of positive energy…. Feeling motivated and encouraged, positive and optimistic… each and every day…

You are safe… in the knowledge that your unconscious mind is always looking out for you…

As every day you are going to experience a greater feeling of well-being, mental as well as physical well-being… a greater feeling of safety and security too than you have felt in a long …long time… allowing you to live your life in a way that is so much more satisfying…satisfying for you…

/

And… Nowww… I will begin to count up from 1 to 10 and with each number, I count up you will become 10 per cent more awake by the count of 8 your eyes will open, and by the count of 10 you will be wide awake and fully alert… and all natural and normal sensations will return to your limbs… and you will wake up feeling, rested, rejuvenated, relaxed, happy, and wonderful, ready for the rest of the day… ready to achieve your ideal weight and your dream body…

So…1…2…3 Drifting towards wakefulness…4…5…6 waking up more and more…7…8…open your eyes… 9… and 10… Wide awake, wide awake…fully wide awake…

Thank you for listening to this powerful hypnosis audio, please remember that the results will continue to increase long after the session has finished. The results get profoundly deeper each time you listen to this recording.

Session 3: Hypnosis Script – Fat Burn & Exercise

Overview: This session will focus on direct suggestions for fat burning and motivation for exercising daily.

Time: 60-minutes

[Reader Notes]

- The rhythm and pace are important therefore please read the following script at a steady pace, ensuring to take your time to guide the listener with your voice.
- Allow long comfortable pauses in between passages that you are happy with, and follow the key set out below to allow longer pauses.
- Embedded commands: Embedded commands will be written in **bold**, the reader must read the bold phrases at a slightly faster pace than the rest of the script. Eg: "See how easy it is to **Just Relax** Nowww", See how easy it is should be ready normally while "just relax" should be read slightly faster returning back to the normal pace when reading "Nowww".
- Nowww: The word "Nowww" should be emphasized and said on an out-breath as if sighing.

[Pause Key]

… Very short pause: Reader pauses for 2 seconds

/ Short pause: Reader pauses for 10 seconds

// Medium pause: Reader pauses for 20 seconds

/// Long pause: Reader pauses for 30 seconds

[Script Begins]

Welcome to the third session in the Weight-loss and Deep Sleep audiobook! A Hypnosis/Guided Meditation series.

This powerful hypnosis audio will focus on suggestions for increased fat burning and motivation for exercising daily.

Begin by finding a comfortable place where you can be alone for just a little while...
You can either sit down comfortably or lie down, please make sure your arms are by your sides and are uncrossed throughout the session.

Now you are in position, bring your awareness to your eyelids and imagine that your eyelids are becoming heavy and tired... heavy and tired... and I wonder how soon it would be before they close... that's right... allow your eyes to close... and now... I would like you to begin tensing the muscles in your face more and more...and as you tense your muscles in your face...hold...and relax those muscles ...allow those muscles to go loose and limp drifting deeper and deeper... as you Nowww... bring your awareness to your neck and begin to tense the muscles in your neck more and more... and Nowww... relax the muscles in your neck... allow them to go loose and limp... loose and limp relaxed... going deeper and deeper...

Guide your awareness now to the muscles of your shoulders, arms, hands, and fingers... tense those muscles more and more... hold the tension... and... relax... allow your shoulders... arms... hands and fingers to now relax... allow them to go loose and limp... loose and limp relaxed...

Nowww... allow your attention to move down to your chest...tensing the muscles in your chest more and more...hold the tension and...relax... allow the muscles of your chest to go loose and limp... loose and limp relaxed...going deeper and deeper Nowww... well done...

Begin to now tense the muscles in your stomach and abdomen... tensing those muscles... hold the tension... and... relax...allow the muscles of the stomach to go loose and limp...loose and limp relaxed...

Moving **down** to the muscles of your hips and buttocks... tense the muscles of your hips and buttocks more and more... hold the tension... and... relax... allow the muscles of your hips and buttocks to relax... and go loose and limp... loose and limp relaxed... going deeper and deeper and you relax...

And Nowww... the muscles of your thighs... tensing them more and more... hold the tension... and... relax... allow the muscles of your thighs to go loose and limp... loose and limp relaxed... going deeper and deeper...

Allow your attention to **go down** into your calves...allow the muscles of your calves to tense more and more... and hold this tension... and... now relax... allow the muscles of your calves to go loose and limp relaxed more and more...

And finally, **move down** to your feet... tensing the muscles in your feet... hold the tension... and relax... allow the muscles in your feet to go loose and limp... loose and limp relaxed... going deeper and deeper...Nowww... you're doing really well...

Begin now to tense all the muscles in your body to the best of your ability from the top of your head to the tips of your toes...tense all your muscles... hold this tension... keep holding....and... relax... **let go** Nowww... allowing yourself to **sink deep** into this relaxation... **sink deep** into this state of peace...

That's right... relaxing more and more...continue to go deeper and deeper... with every word that I say... and soon you may begin to find that every sound... guides you deeper... every thought... guides you deeper... every breath in... and every breath out... guides you deeper and deeper... and even... every heartbeat guides you deeper and deeper still... so simply **let go** now... let go Nowww...

So... I would like you to imagine that you are standing on top of a spiral staircase that is going down... the staircase has 10 steps... imagine yourself there... on top of that spiral staircase... and in a moment I will begin to count down from 10 to 1 and with each descending number from 10 and 1 I would like you to start walking down these stairs... to my count... and notice how with each descending number I count down from 10 to 1 you are going 10 times deeper than you have ever been before...

So ready... 10... Going deeper and deeper...9... Feeling better and better...with each step you take down these stairs... 8 ... The deeper you go the better you feel... 7... The better you feel the deeper you go... with each step you walk down these stairs... 6... drifting ever more deeper still... moving closer and closer to the bottom of the stairs... and 5... feeling a sense of safety and security and 4... feeling a sense of optimism taking over you and you become open to change and transformation... 3 ... feeling free... 2... you are almost there... and...1... you are doing really well...

Very good... Nowww imagine a bright light shining down from above melting away all of the excess fat on your body... imagine it flowing down off you... it will feel pleasant and wonderful... as you become lighter and lighter... this will remind your unconscious mind why you are here... and soon I will begin to countdown from 10 to 1 and with each number I count down... I would like you to notice yourself going even deeper and deeper and the excess weight begins to trickle down your body reaching the ground, leaving that lighter, healthier slimmer version of yourself... that was always there within... so... ready... 10... allow that excess fat... that excess weight to begin melting off as you go deeper and deeper still... 9... that's it more and more... going deeper and deeper... as that light cleanses you and heals whatever is underneath that excess fat as it melts off... 8... drifting ever more deeper still with every word that I say...7 ... imagining the excess fat reaching the ground as you go even deeper and deeper... 6... more and more deeper still with each passing moment that's right... 5...letting go... letting go of any resistance that may develop... as you go deeper and deeper... 4... letting go of any deep-rooted limiting beliefs that are preventing change... 3... feeling the freedom as you begin to feel lighter and lighter as all that excess weight begins to melt off you... 2...almost done... all of that weight is almost completely melted off you...and.... Nowww... 1... well done... all that excess weight has now melted off you as you are now free ... free from that excess weight... free from limiting beliefs and free from any resistances... very good... continue to go deeper and deeper ... more and more... solidify this message within your unconscious mind ... pave the way to inner transformation... to reach your weight goals and melt away that excess fat to reveal the healthier... slimmer... thinner version of yourself that was always there... so... Nowww... that we have set the stage... let us begin...

You are open and ready to **begin exercising** now... every day you will feel a sense of excitement to **start exercising** daily... imagine going back in time... back in time to a memory where you were really excited to do something... or go somewhere... perhaps to carry out a specific task... I will give you a moment of time to return back to this memory...

//

See what you were seeing... perhaps noticing the sounds around you... becoming aware of whether you were indoors or outdoors... alone or with someone... becoming aware of what it was you were excited to be doing... notice how it feels to **be excited**... to look forward to doing something... feel those sensations rush through your body....

And Nowww... I would like you to imagine a dial... very similar to a dial you would find on a radio which can be used to increase or decrease the volume... Imagine this dial...and it's currently set on 1...and it goes up to 10... in a moment I will begin counting up from 1 to 10 and with each number I count up... I would like you to turn up this dial notch by notch to my count... and notice that as you begin to turn up this dial to my count... each number I count up will cause those feelings of excitement to become stronger and stronger... so ready... grab hold of that dial... imagine it between your fingertips... turn up those feelings of excitement... Nowww... 1...2... feel those feelings of excitement increase more and more...3...turning up those feelings... 4... allow those feelings of excitement to grow... 5... filling your entire body as it increases... 6... filling you from the tips of your toes up to the top of your head...7... that's right... allow those feelings to grow... 8 ...feeling excited more and more...9... those feelings are almost at its peak... and... 10... allow the excitement to burst through you...

As soon as you wake up every morning and think about exercising all these feelings of excitement will return to you instantly and easily and you'll be filled with an immense urge to exercise…

It doesn't matter where you are… as soon as you wake up every morning and think about exercising all these feelings of excitement will return to you instantly and easily and you'll be filled with an immense urge to exercise…

Exercising will become more and more enjoyable each time you think about it… and after every workout, you will be more excited for the next session of physical exercise… You feel an immense sense of motivation to **begin immediately** now….

You know that as soon as you **begin exercising** daily… all you need to do is **continue exercising daily**… and you will begin to come closer and closer to your desired weight… and you are filled with excitement to make this a reality for you… because as soon as you wake up every morning and think about exercising, all these feelings of excitement will return to you instantly and easily and you'll be filled with an immense urge to exercise…

Your unconscious mind will begin to help your body…burn that excess fat… quicker and quicker every time… after every workout, your unconscious mind… facilitates the internal processes of the body to begin burning your excess fat at a quicker pace… and to ensure this process takes place at its optimum level you **exercise daily**… and **it is easy to exercise daily** Nowww… because you now know that as soon as you wake up every morning… and think about exercising all these feelings of excitement will return to you instantly and easily… and you'll be filled with an immense urge to exercise…

And Nowww… I would like your unconscious mind… the part of you that is responsible for motivation… that part of you that is responsible for excitement and the part of you which will ensure that as soon as you wake up every morning… and think about exercising, all these feelings of excitement will return to you instantly and easily… and you'll be filled with an immense urge to exercise… I would like your unconscious mind to relay this message to every part of you… to all of your bones… your ligaments… your muscles… all your cells… and all aspects of yourself, that **you are someone who exercises daily** Nowww…

You are someone who enjoys exercising now… and looks forward to a good session of exercise every single day… you do not feel quite right if you skip a session… you must exercise daily and feel the urge to exercise every single day…because… as soon as you wake up every morning and think about exercising all these feelings of excitement will return to you instantly and easily and you'll be filled with an immense urge to exercise… very good… you are doing really well…

And I will give you just a moment of time which is all the time you need to just relax… and this will also assist all my suggestions to **sink deep** into your unconscious mind…

///

And... Nowww...I would like to thank your unconscious mind for its cooperation... and before I awaken you... I want you to know that... as each day goes by you are going to become a little more mentally calm... a little more clear in your mind... each and every day... which means that you will see things more clearly... think more clearly... so that no-one and nothing will ever be able to affect you or upset you in quite the same way.. your mind becomes clearer and clearer... crystal clear... allowing you to feel physically calm and relaxed too... not only in your body but you will also feel more emotionally calm and more relaxed about yourself... and about the world around you...

And you can enjoy these feelings of well-being each and every day no matter what you're doing, where you are or who you're with and you will find that you are going to feel fitter and stronger in every way... feeling more energetic... feeling more alert... enjoying a greater and greater sense of positive energy.... Feeling motivated and encouraged, positive and optimistic... each and every day...
You are safe... in the knowledge that your unconscious mind is always looking out for you...

Every day...you will feel a positive sense of strength... your mind clearer and calmer... tranquil... serene and focused and as the days...weeks ...and months go by and you feel ever more calm and relaxed in your mind and body...you will find that you think more clearly... concentrate more effectively... giving your whole undivided attention to whatever you are doing... and consequently, you will be able to see things in their truest perspective... and you become emotionally calmer... every day you remain more and more relaxed physically, emotionally, and mentally...coping appropriately with each and every situation you handle in your daily life...

As every day you are going to experience a greater feeling of well-being, mental as well as physical well-being... a greater feeling of safety and security too than you have felt in a long ...long time... allowing you to live your life in a way that is so much more satisfying...satisfying for you...

/

And... Nowww... I will begin to count up from 1 to 10 and with each number, I count up you will become 10 percent more awake by the count of 8 your eyes will open, and by the count of 10 you will be wide awake and fully alert... and all natural and normal sensations will return to your limbs... and you will wake up feeling, rested, rejuvenated, relaxed, happy, and wonderful, ready for the rest of the day... ready to achieve your ideal weight and your dream body...

So…1…2…3 Drifting towards wakefulness…4…5…6 waking up more and more…7…8…open your eyes… 9… and 10… Wide awake, wide awake…fully wide awake…

Thank you for listening to this powerful hypnosis audio, please remember that the results will continue to increase long after the session has finished. The results get profoundly deeper each time you listen to this recording.

Session 4: Hypnosis Script – Self-love & Integration

Overview: This session will focus on reconnecting the listener to self-love by using parts dissociation therapy and sealing off the sessions with self-integration work.

Time: 60-minutes

[Reader Notes]

- The rhythm and pace are important therefore please read the following script at a steady pace, ensuring to take your time to guide the listener with your voice.
- Allow long comfortable pauses in between passages that you are happy with, and follow the key set out below to allow longer pauses.
- Embedded commands: Embedded commands will be written in **bold**, the reader must read the bold phrases at a slightly faster pace than the rest of the script. Eg: "See how easy it is to **Just Relax** Nowww", See how easy it is should be ready normally while "just relax" should be read slightly faster returning back to the normal pace when reading "Nowww".
- Nowww: The word "Nowww" should be emphasized and said on an out-breath as if sighing.

[Pause Key]

… Very short pause: Reader pauses for 2 seconds

/ Short pause: Reader pauses for 10 seconds

// Medium pause: Reader pauses for 20 seconds

/// Long pause: Reader pauses for 30 seconds

_____

[Script Begins]

Welcome to the fourth session in the Weight-loss and Deep Sleep audiobook! A Hypnosis/Guided Meditation series.

This powerful hypnosis audio will focus on reconnecting you to self-love and reinforcing the work we have done in the previous sessions.

Begin by finding a comfortable place where you can be alone for just a little while...
You can either sit down comfortably or lie down, please make sure your arms are by your sides and are uncrossed throughout the session.

Now you are in position, take a deep breath in through your nose... and let it out... Nowwww... relax... and simply... allow your eyes to close... that's right... returning back... returning back into that state of peace... into that state of calm soothing relaxation... where you can **let go** more and more... drifting deeper and deeper with every word that I say...and soon you may begin to find that every sound... guides you deeper... every thought... guides you deeper... every breath in... and every breath out... guides you deeper and deeper... and even... every heartbeat guides you deeper and deeper still... so simply **let go** now... let go Nowww...

So... I would like you to imagine that you are standing on top of a hill with a long path that is going down... imagine yourself there... on top of that hill... and in a moment I will begin to count down from 10 to 1 and with each descending number from 10 to 1 I would like you to start walking down this path... to my count... and notice how with each descending number I count down from 10 to 1 you are going 10 times deeper than you have ever been before... So ready... 10... Going deeper and deeper...9... Feeling better and better...with each step you take down this hill ... 8 ... The deeper you go the better you feel... 7... The better you feel the deeper you go... with each step you walk down this path... 6... drifting ever more deeper still... moving closer and closer to the bottom of the hill... and 5... feeling a sense of safety and security and 4... feeling a sense of optimism taking over you and you become open to change and transformation... 3 ... feeling free... 2... you are almost there... and...1...

...you're doing very well.. remain deeply relaxed and imagine that now there is a very magical looking door that appears in the field below...the door leads to a very special room...

It is a beautifully decorated room of learning... a room of learning which will have a large whiteboard on the wall...

So open that door… and walk into this room… see what you would see… perhaps noticing if there are any items in this room… noticing the whiteboard… perhaps being aware of any sounds that would be present here…

I want you Nowww… to go over to the whiteboard… quite close by I would like you to find a white board marker pen and an eraser… I want you Nowww… to stand in front of the whiteboard… I want you to take the marker pen and write the number 5 at the top of the board… as you begin to draw… notice how you form the number 5… see the number 5 on the whiteboard … now when you can see the 5 … I want you to take the eraser and wipe it away… wipe away the number 5… breathe and relax… Very Good…

Nowww… write on the board with the marker… the words **deep sleep**… and as you write these words clearly… allow yourself to go 20 times deeper and deeper… Nowww…

Wipe these words clean off the board using the eraser and allow your mind to clear… as you now begin to write the number 4 on the board… until you can see it clearly… and Nowww… erase the number 4… wipe it away… breathe and relax…

Nowww… write on the board with the marker… the words **let go**… and as you write these words clearly… allow yourself to go 20 times deeper and deeper… Nowww…
Wipe these words clean off the board using the eraser and allow your mind to clear… as you now begin to write the number 3 on the board… until you can see it clearly… and Nowww… erase the number 3… wipe it away… breathe and relax…

Nowww… write on the board with the marker… the words **Drifting deeper**… and as you write these words clearly… allow yourself to go 20 times deeper and deeper… Nowww…

Wipe these words clean off the board using the eraser and allow your mind to clear… as you now begin to write the number 2 on the board… until you can see it clearly… and Nowww… erase the number 2… wipe it away… breathe and relax… That's right…

Nowww… write on the board with the marker… the words **deeply relaxed**… and as you write these words clearly… allow yourself to go 20 times deeper and deeper… Nowww…

Wipe these words clean off the board using the eraser and allow your mind to clear… as you now begin to write the number 1 on the board… until you can see it clearly… and Nowww… erase the number 1… wipe it away… breathe and relax… you are doing really well…

And... Now... Nowww... write on the board with the marker... the words **let go completely**... and as you write these words clearly... allow yourself to go 20 times deeper and deeper... Nowww...

However... this time when you wipe these words off... allow your mind to go blank... as you drift 30 times deeper and deeper... Nowww...

You are very... very deeply relaxed... allow yourself to relax deeper... and deeper still... listen carefully to the things that I tell you... and ask of you... because everything I say will happen... it will happen exactly as I describe... let your inner mind absorb my words and suggestions ... they will become part of your reality so that the positive effects will also be a reality for you... you will be able to talk and respond to me when asked and you will remain completely relaxed and in trance...

And... Nowww... I would like to speak with your unconscious mind about a matter of importance, important to you...
I would like you to know that if this session gets interrupted in any way that your unconscious mind will ensure that all parts of you will naturally be reintegrated within yourself...

/

I would like your unconscious mind... the part of you that has the answer to all problems... the part of you that has access to all parts of you... to go searching within yourself for the part of you that is lacking or blocking self-love...

And I would like your unconscious mind to bring this part out and float it above your left hand...

/

Notice what this part may look like... perhaps it has a sound... or perhaps it has a feeling... or maybe even all three... however **this part manifests to you** now... become aware of it for a moment...

//

We shall refer to this part as the problem part… I would like you to now ask this problem part for insight as to what it is really doing for you…why is it really here… take a moment to interact with this part in this way Nowww…

//

Nowww… let this part know… that whatever this part needs to **reconnect to self-love** now… there is another part of you that has exactly what this part needs to **reconnect to self-love** now…

//

Let this part know that you will now go searching for the part of you that has exactly what that parts need to **reconnect to self-love** …

//

So Nowww… I would like you to thank the problem part and leave it be for the moment above your left hand…

And I would now like your unconscious mind to go searching within yourself for the part of you that has the solution… the part of you that has exactly what this part needs to **reconnect to self-love** now…

And I would like your unconscious mind to bring this part out and float it above your right hand…

/

Notice what this part may look like… perhaps it has a sound… or perhaps it has a feeling… or maybe even all three… however **this part manifests to you** now… become aware of it for a moment…

//

We shall refer to this part as the solution part… I would like you to now ask this solution part for insight as to what it will do for you… take a moment to interact with this part in this way Nowww…

//

I would like you to thank this part for its insight… and now I will begin to count up from 1 to 5 and with each number I count up, this solution part will become stronger…and stronger… and on the count of 5, this solution part will be 10 times stronger than the problem part…

So ready… 1… increasing the strength of the solution part… 2 more and more… 3 the solution part is already much stronger than the problem part… 4… and … 5 the solution part is now 10 times stronger than the problem part…

Become aware of any changes that may have occurred during the strengthening process of the solution part…

//

And Now… in whatever way is appropriate for you… put the two parts together… merge the problem part with the solution part…

Since the solution is 10 times stronger than the problem… the solution part engulfs the problem part giving it exactly what it needs to **reconnect to self-love** now…

As these two parts now merge… it forms a third unified part which is now floating in the centre in between your hands…

/

Notice what this unified part may look like… perhaps it has a sound… or perhaps it has a feeling… or maybe even all three… however **this part manifests to you** now… become aware of it for a moment…

//

I would like you to thank this part for whatever it will do for you…

//

And Nowww… I would like you to reintegrate this part back within yourself… I will give you a moment of time to carry this out…

//

Very good... Nowww... We all have skin that very clearly separates that which is inside of us... from that which is outside of us... just like the skin on our body, it separates our blood vessels, internal organs, and bones from that which is outside of us...

Similarly, our mind also has a skin that separates that which is inside of us from that which is outside of us... like a boundary... for some people it may be as if they have a circle around them... some people may find it to be like being encased in a bubble...or a force field... or even a shell...

I wonder what your mental skin... your boundary would look like... I wonder whether it would have a particular sound... I wonder what size it would be... I wonder what it would be made out of... I will go silent for a little while... giving you a moment of time which is all the time you need to imagine what your boundary would be like...

//

Nowww... in whatever shape or form your boundary has manifested in... I would like you to imagine that there is a little door in your boundary which you can open and close to let things in and push things out...

You have complete control over what comes in and what goes out of your boundary...

/

And Nowww... I would like you to imagine that within your boundary are parts of yourself that are no longer serving you... that in fact are causing detriment to you... allow your unconscious mind to guide you... and you know intuitively what parts you need to push out of your boundary... I will give you a moment of time to locate these aspects...

/

Nowww... imagine opening the door to your boundary and pushing these detrimental parts out of your boundary, away from you... pushing these detrimental aspects that are no longer serving you right out of your boundary...

/

And Nowww... I would like you to imagine that outside of your boundary are parts of yourself that are in fact useful to you... parts of yourself that are beneficial to your well-being...

Allow your unconscious mind to guide you... and you intuitively know what these aspects are... I will give you a moment of time to locate these aspects...

/

And Nowww... in whatever way is appropriate for you I would like you to pull in these aspects of yourself... inside your boundary... pulling in all these useful... empowering aspects within your boundary...

/

Close the door to your boundary now... only you can open and close this door...
In a moment I will begin to count up from 1 to 10 and with each number I count up I would like your boundary to become stronger and stronger in every way... improving in every way... for your current needs... reinforcing... strengthening...

1... improving your boundary more and more... 2 becoming stronger... 3 becoming reinforced... 4... more and more ...5 go deeper and deeper as this process takes place... 6... 7... 8... improving your boundary... 9... it's almost complete... and... 10...

Become aware of your new and improved boundary... notice what it looks like... notice if it has a particular sound or feeling associated with it... notice what its size is... notice what it is made out of...

/

Whenever you need a sense of self-control and strength... you will naturally become aware of your boundary.. formulating around you... filling you with strength and self-control... this process will happen naturally and unconsciously... filling you with all the positive qualities provided by the positive aspects of yourself that you have pulled into your boundary...

/

Nowww... simply allow the boundary to fade away... knowing that it is always in place... providing you with these inner positive qualities...

And Nowww... I will give you just a moment of time, which is all the time you need, to just relax and enjoy this state, and this will also assist all my suggestions to **sink deep** into your unconscious mind...

///

And... Nowww...I would like to thank your unconscious mind for its cooperation...
Each and every day no matter what you're doing, where you are or who you're with and you will find that you are going to feel fitter and stronger in every way... feeling more energetic... feeling more alert... enjoying a greater and greater sense of positive energy.... Feeling motivated and encouraged, positive and optimistic... each and every day...

You are safe... in the knowledge that your unconscious mind is always looking out for you...

Every day...you will feel a positive sense of strength... your mind clearer and calmer... tranquil... serene and focused and as the days...weeks ...and months go by and you feel ever more calm and relaxed in your mind and body...you will find that you think more clearly... concentrate more effectively... giving your whole undivided attention to whatever you are doing...

As every day you are going to experience a greater feeling of well-being, mental as well as physical well-being... a greater feeling of safety and security too than you have felt in a long ...long time... allowing you to live your life in a way that is so much more satisfying...satisfying for you...

/

And... Nowww... I will begin to count up from 1 to 10 and with each number, I count up you will become 10 percent more awake by the count of 8 your eyes will open, and by the count of 10 you will be wide awake and fully alert... and all natural and normal sensations will return to your limbs... and you will wake up feeling, rested, rejuvenated, relaxed, happy, and wonderful, ready for the rest of the day... ready to achieve your ideal weight and your dream body...

So...1...2...3 Drifting towards wakefulness...4...5...6 waking up more and more...7...8...open your eyes... 9... and 10... Wide awake, wide awake...fully wide awake...

Thank you for listening to this powerful hypnosis audio, please remember that the results will continue to increase long after the session has finished. The results get profoundly deeper each time you listen to this recording.

Session 5: Guided Meditation - Overcoming Insomnia

Time: 30 mins

[Reader Notes]

- Read the following script at a steady pace, taking your time to guide the meditator/listener with your voice.
- Allow comfortable pauses that you are happy with, and follow the key set out below to allow longer pauses.

[Pause Key]

/ Short pause: The reader takes a long breath.
// Medium pause: The reader pauses for 30 seconds.
/// Long pause: The reader pauses for 2 minutes +

[Meditation Begins]

Welcome to this guided meditation for overcoming insomnia as you continue on your weight loss journey brought to you by.

Begin this guided meditation before you get into bed. Overcoming insomnia is a process, and research shows that you are more likely to enjoy quality rest and even sleep by beginning with a bedtime ritual.

/

You see, Insomnia is a sleep disorder that affects at least 50% of adults at least once in their lifetime. When we become overly stressed, anxious, fearful or even overly stimulated, it can prove difficult to enjoy good quality sleep. Sleep is a vital component of the weight loss journey, and so by listening to this guided meditation, you can begin to overcome insomnia and increase your weight loss as a result.

/
Standing next to your bed, take a few deep breaths.
Now is a good time to centre yourself in this moment.

Before you climb into bed, bring your awareness to the tiredness in the body right now.

/

Your mental checklist will pop up soon.
Allow your mind to scan the list.
Closed the window, check.

Front door locked, check.

Garden lights off, check.

Alarm set, check.

/

Allow any last-minute thoughts to pass.
What am I going to wear tomorrow?

Wonder if I'll get a seat on the train.

I must try and eat healthily tomorrow.

Like clouds in the sky, your thoughts may keep coming,
One after the other, morphing into new thoughts,
Creeping across the sky, slowly drifting away,
Until eventually, they pass in their usual monotonous way.

//

Dim the lights if you haven't already done so.
Make sure the temperature of the room is just right.

Scribble down any last-minute tasks or lingering ideas.

Close your laptop.

Silence your mobile phone.

Put any other screens away.

And snuggle down beneath the sheets.

Permitting yourself to relax

///

Allow your thoughts to turn to gratitude.
What are you grateful for today?

A nice cup of coffee this morning.

A great conversation with your colleague at work.

A funny joke told by a friend.

A heartwarming story on Facebook.

Allow your gratitude to expand as you relax.
Letting the feelings of gratitude and calm spread throughout your body.

///

Now that you have completed your bedtime ritual
You can relax and let go as you lie down,
Feel the body assume its usual resting position.
Allow the breath to cultivate relaxation in the body and mind.

/

As you breathe in, feel the lungs fill with air.
When you exhale, feel the body soften into your mattress.
Picture yourself falling deeper into the mattress as the body relaxes with each exhale.
Lie on your back with your arms relaxed by your sides.
Take a moment to get comfortable.
Slowly close your eyes, or focus on one spot on the floor or wall.
Invite your body and mind to begin to relax.

///

Our brains benefit from quality sleep, our bodies benefit from quality sleep, and those around us benefit when we enjoy a good night's sleep. Quality sleep helps with focus and attention; it helps with clarity and emotional intelligence. There is nothing that cannot be achieved following a good night's sleep.

[Quote]
"William Shakespeare once said, Let her sleep for when she wakes she will move mountains."

As you wind down now,
Everything is taken care of.

As you close your eyes,
Allow the muscles around the eyes to relax.

Allow your head to sink deeply into the pillow.
Let your arms and shoulders fall.

Allow the breath to soften your back.
Loosen the hips and pelvis.

And as you exhale, let your ankles, feet and knees relax.
Just relaxing deeper with every breath you take.

///

Allow any thoughts of worry or the passing day to just be present in your mind.
There is no need to push them away or stop them.
Take a nice relaxing deep breath in.
And as you exhale, drop your shoulders down,
release your hands, fingers and jaw.
Close your eyes and drop your brow, now breathe.

///

As you breathe at your regular pace,
bring your full awareness to your thoughts.

Perhaps there are thoughts of worrying about your weight.
Maybe you are afraid that you won't lose the weight.
Perhaps you are concerned that you are not losing weight fast enough.
Whatever your thoughts are at this time,
There is no need to push or pull them in any direction.
There is no need to challenge your thoughts at all.
Just observe and identify any pressing ideas about your weight or anything else.

///

If your thoughts become overwhelming, simply take a breath.
Now return your full awareness to noticing the breath,
then allow your attention to drift to your thoughts once again.
Following any thoughts, seeing where your mind may wander,
take a few moments to notice your worries,
there is no need to judge them or alter them in any way,
just observe them.

//

When we begin to notice how much we worry,
when we worry, and why we worry,
we can begin to release our worries.
So, using the breath to guide you,
once again, follow your mind,
as it wanders towards your fears,
and just observe whatever you find there.

///

[Quote]
"Worrying is using your imagination to create something you don't want - Abraham Hicks."

The imagination is a powerful tool that can help us to create stories in our minds,
many of which are worries about the future.

When we become concerned about losing weight or a lack of weight loss, this can cause insomnia, anxiety and even depression.

Did you know that 5 - 10% of worries are problems that we can solve, and most of our fears never actually materialise; they are often just the result of our vivid imaginations?

//

Become aware of these worries or concerns about your weight, and remind yourself that many of these worries are simply imagined worries.
The good news is that now you can begin to release these worries and enjoy a good night's sleep; as you know, sleep is an essential component of weight loss.
So by releasing these figments of your imagination, you will begin to overcome insomnia and boost your weight loss journey.

///

Focus on your breathing, once again following your breath,
as it comes into your body and goes out of your body.
Imagine that with each breath in; you're breathing in drowsiness and relaxation,
and with each breath out, you're releasing racing thoughts and weight loss worries.

Now, return your awareness to your breathing.
And take a long deep breath in.
Enjoy breathing and filling the body and mind with fresh, rejuvenating air.
And now, I would like you to redirect your imagination as I take you on a journey.

///

Now I am going to take you on a guided visualisation journey.
One where all you have to do is listen to my voice and relax.
And as you join me on this journey, I will guide you into a state of rest.
Where even if you do not fall asleep,
your body will still get the rest it needs to accelerate your weight loss.

///

Continue breathing deeply another five times.
Making sure to breathe out fully and completely.
As you make way for a fresh breath coming in each time.
///

The mind is just like the sun.
Each morning the mind awakens like the sun rising in the sky,
at night, the mind relaxes just as the sun sets on the horizon.
Imagine sitting outside in a comfortable chair, now
a little before sunset, and you're facing in the direction of the setting sun.
Notice if there are clouds in the sky,
Now begin to notice the colours you see in the sky.
As the sun is just starting to set, imagine seeing different shades of red in the sky.
As you begin to relax the mind, imagine seeing that red in the sky fade to a softer orange.
As the light slowly continues to fade in the sky,
allow your mind to slow down, and begin to relax deeply.
Imagine your body becoming more comfortable as the colour fades in the sky.
And slowly, you start to see some pinks in between the soft orange colours.
Notice how gentle and calm your mind feels now.
As the sun continues to set,
you might see some soft purple hues in the sky.
Imagine your body becoming more and more comfortable,
letting any distractions fade just as the colours in the sky are fading.

//

Notice the sky becoming slightly darker,
Imagine your mind continuing to relax.
Notice that the sun is just about gone now,
as your mind surrenders to the comfort of rest.

///

Now, you can invite your body and mind
to continue to feel comfortable and relaxed,
even as your attention drifts elsewhere.
Clear any last thoughts as your mind slows down,
as you drift, just drifting into deep relaxation.

Your mind can continue to slow down,
as your body finds comfort in the soft cosy bed
and just as the colours in the sunset have faded,
this meditation draws to a close.
Sweet dreams.

Session 6: Guided Meditation - Self Love & Weight Loss

Time: 30 mins

[Reader Notes]

- Read the following script at a steady pace, taking your time to guide the meditator/listener with your voice.
- Allow comfortable pauses that you are happy with, and follow the key set out below to allow longer pauses.

[Pause Key]

/ Short pause: The reader takes a long breath.
// Medium pause: The reader pauses for 30 seconds.
/// Long pause: The reader pauses for 2 minutes +

[Meditation Begins]

Welcome to this guided meditation for increasing self love and weight loss brought to you by _____.

Hello and welcome to this guided meditation, where you will experience a strong sense of self-love as you enter into relaxation. We all know how important rest and sleep are for weight loss, but how often do you consider the part that self-love and acceptance play in your weight loss journey?

One of the reasons that many people regain the weight they lose is due to a need for protection or a negative self-image. Some people simply do not believe they deserve to be slim and healthy, while others feel safer and more comfortable when they are heavier and more vulnerable when they are thinner.

So, although you may express a desire to lose weight, sometimes the subconscious beliefs you hold can cause you to hold onto it.

The following meditation will assist you in accepting your body in its natural slimmer healthier state, and help you to increase your inner strength and power.

So when you are ready and feel comfortable and supported, we can begin the meditation.

///

You are about to embark on a guided meditation journey, where I will guide you into a deep state of relaxation in which you will experience a calmness and meditative state of mind.

This time is for you and you alone, and all you have to do is relax and allow yourself to have this time and do whatever feels suitable for you as you relax.

And now, I would simply like you to focus on your breath.

Breathe in deeply

Exhale fully

Breathe in deeply

Exhale fully

Breathe in deeply

Exhale fully

//

You may notice some thoughts and self-talk in your mind; that's okay, allow them to pass by, and they will slow down as you concentrate on listening to the sounds in the background.

/

And now, as you breathe deeply, you will find that your mind gently begins to quiet.

Breath in deeply

Exhale fully

Breathing in the cool refreshing air

Exhaling any negative, warm, tense air

The more you listen, the more relaxed you feel.

Allow yourself to be in total peace with your surroundings.

Now, as you relax, calm your mind.

Breathe deeply

Exhale fully

Feel the incredible sense of deep relaxation wash over you, calming and soothing

And now I would like you to join me on a journey.

A journey deep into your imagination, are you ready?

/

And now you see yourself in a beautiful garden.
A private garden where you are the only one in the garden.
This garden is exotic. It has palm trees and birds singing in the trees.
As you begin to walk through the garden, you notice a light warm breeze and the sun starting to set.
It's calm and quiet apart from the sound of the birds singing.
The leaves bristle on the breeze, and in the distance, you hear the sound of water.

///

As you walk towards the sound, eventually you come to a clearing, and in the clearing, you notice a vast waterfall. It is, in fact, the most impressive waterfall you have ever seen.

///

And as you stand in front of the waterfall, you see a bench and decide to sit.
Listening to the sound of the waterfall is a new experience.

It is as if the intense rushing sound of the water as you sit up close is somehow penetrating your mind and your body.
Every cell reverberates with the pounding of the water as it hits the rocks beneath it. The smell is vibrant and fresh. The energy is powerful and breathtaking.

///

The wonder of being here with this waterfall affects every sense.
The sight, the sound, the sensation, the smell, it's all so beautiful and yet so intimidating.

///

This moment is the moment where you release all of your thoughts of judgement, self-doubt and loathing to the power of the waterfall.
Allow each of them to be emptied from your mind into the rushing intensity of the water. Allow the waterfall to rush them away, pound them on the rocks beneath it to dissolve them into nothingness. Let them go.

///

And now imagine the intensity of the pounding water pushing away the tension you feel in your body.
You are allowing the tension to be pummeled out of your body by the power of the waterfall. Let every part of your body be relieved of the stress or anxiety that has caused you to gain weight. Let your mind be cleansed of the self-critical words of hate and disgust.
Surrender it all to the power of the waterfall.
You are safe here. All is secure so that you can surrender. Remember this is your safe place, where nobody can enter; it's just you and the cleansing power of your waterfall.

///

Now notice how the longer you sit, the more your concerns and doubts about life are washed away. See how any doubts you had about your ability to release weight are washed away. Notice how any doubts you ever had about being slim and toned and healthy are rushed away in the avalanche of water.

///

Let go of all negative thoughts, release them into the waterfall, allowing you to make space for new, positive thoughts and beliefs, for unlimited beliefs that will serve you in your journey of weight loss. Replace the negative with positive as you allow any doubts about your healthy, fit body and future weight management to simply dissolve into the rigorous flow of the waterfall.

///

Now is the time to throw in any doubts about your ability to release excess fat through healthy eating and exercise and have them washed away.
Release any beliefs that it's hard to lose weight or tone and improve your physical body and allow them to be washed away.

Replace those thoughts with thoughts of confidence that you do lose weight now.

Throw into the waterfall any thoughts or beliefs of excess weight being protective or suitable for you and watch as they are rushed away by the relentless flow of the waterfall.

Replace these with great thoughts of how weight loss is improving your life and making everything better.

///

For the first time in a long time, tell yourself you are sure, you are confident that losing weight is a beautiful new experience for you.
Weight loss brings new and happy experiences.
Weight loss is the key to a safe and protected life.
Weight loss brings you much of the joy and happiness that you seek in life.
Weight loss is a positive change in your life.

///

I want you to know that you are good enough to let the weight go.
You are better without it.
You have the inner strength to protect yourself.
You are more vital when you are fitter.
You are truly capable of achieving all of your weight loss goals quickly.

///

I want you to know that you are powerful and beautiful.
You are strong and healthy.
You are sexy and divine.
You think and feel positive thoughts and feelings about your body right now.
You are sure and secure about your body without the extra weight.
You are confident that life is better without excess weight.

///

And as you look around this beautiful exotic paradise sat in front of this powerful waterfall, you wonder at the power of the water and the ability to wash away the negative and replace it with the positive.

Just before we bring this meditation to a close,
repeat these affirmations after me;

I love myself
I accept myself
I am worthy of self-love
I am worthy of a slim and toned body
I am worthy of a lean and healthy body
I am strong enough to protect myself
I love myself
I am proud of myself
I am doing a good job every day of my life
I am putting myself and my needs first every day
I love my weight loss journey
I am in love with myself and my body
I am a beautiful and powerful person
I have an unshakeable belief in my body
I am making the best healthy weight loss choices daily
I always attract only the most nutritious foods
I engage in only the most positive habits and activities
I love and appreciate every part of my body
I am proud of the way I look
I am full of health, strength, beauty and vitality

///

And again

I love myself
I accept myself
I am worthy of self-love
I am worthy of a slim and toned body
I am worthy of a lean and healthy body
I am strong enough to protect myself
I love myself
I am proud of myself
I am doing a good job every day of my life
I am putting myself and my needs first every day
I love my weight loss journey
I am in love with myself and my body
I am a beautiful and powerful person
I have an unshakeable belief in my body
I am making the best healthy weight loss choices daily
I always attract only the most nutritious foods
I engage in only the most positive habits and activities

I love and appreciate every part of my body
I am proud of the way I look
I am full of health, strength, beauty and vitality

///

And you know that you can return at any time to your safe place alone.
Whenever you notice those doubts or negative self-talk creeping back in, listen to this guided meditation again and surrender those thoughts to the waterfall.

This is your special secret safe, peaceful place where you can relax, just sit beside the waterfall where there is no judgement, no pressure, no stress, only peace, calm and the sounds and smells of this beautiful exotic hideaway.

///

Whenever you need to experience a positive moment where you can impress thoughts of well-being and goodness on your subconscious, you know you can return to the waterfall.

You understand that this is the place where you make your best decisions, develop your best beliefs, where you enjoy your thoughts of love, positivity and self-belief; you are reminded of your true beauty, and you feel your power.

///

Just like the power of the waterfall, you can give yourself the gift of being in the moment and having perfect inner peace, the place where you feel satisfied with your life because you know your life is the ideal journey for you and you know that everything is working together for your good.

///

And then, as the waterfall continues in the background, you begin to sense your thoughts slowly coming back, and you become aware of your breath once again, and you slowly rise to your feet.

As you walk back to the exit of the private garden, you continue to feel beautiful, powerful and confident, and as you return to the thoughts of the evening ahead, you feel healthy, strong and sure of your weight loss journey improving your life.

You can be sure that this is your rightful state, slim, toned and healthy.

As we near the end of this session, take a moment to reflect on what you have just experienced. Hopefully, you managed to follow my guidance throughout this meditation and practised releasing all of the negative thoughts and doubts that you held about weight loss.

/

Whatever you noticed from today's meditation, you can be proud of the fact that you are well on your way to losing weight and increasing your sense of self-love and acceptance.

/

When you're ready, take a long, slow breath in and as you exhale, open your eyes or lift your gaze, wiggle your fingers and toes, and gently come back to the room.

/

Remember, meditation is a practice, and just like any other skill, it requires effort and repetition.

Once this meditation is over, as you go about the rest of your day or evening, see if you can take brief moments to practice releasing any negative thoughts about weight loss or yourself.

Whenever you do manage to release these thoughts, practice replacing them with a positive life-affirming thought in its place.

Session 7: Guided Meditation - Deep Sleep For Rapid Weight Loss

Time: 60 mins

[Reader Notes]

- Read the following script at a steady pace, taking your time to guide the meditator/listener with your voice.
- Allow comfortable pauses that you are happy with, and follow the key set out below to allow longer pauses.

[Pause Key]

/ Short pause: The reader takes a long breath.
// Medium pause: The reader pauses for 30 seconds.
/// Long pause: The reader pauses for 2 minutes +

[Meditation Begins]

Welcome to this guided meditation for Deep Sleep and Rapid Weight Loss, brought to you by _____.

Welcome, dear friends….it is such a pleasure to have you join me on this deep sleep rapid weight loss guided meditation.

It is time to relax, unwind, and leave the day behind.

And as you get ready for a good night's rest, take a few deep breaths and just tell yourself that now is a good time to lay back, relax and take a mental vacation to the beach.

/

And as you make yourself comfortable, loosening any tight clothing, adjusting your position to one of comfort and support, it's time to drift off to your very own private Caribbean island where you will find a luxury beach hut waiting just for you.

///

So as we begin, set your intentions for deep relaxation - rapid weight loss overnight and a good night's sleep.

///

And as you ponder on the day that has just gone by or even the day ahead, allow your thoughts to slow and your mind to be at ease.

And as you look forward to a night of rest and repair for your body and your mind you can be optimistic about the good night's sleep that lies ahead.

//

And now, you are here with me, anticipating your journey into sleep. We can begin with some deep relaxation techniques to help you to release the tension and tightness that you may have developed throughout the day, these techniques will cause rapid weight loss.

///

So close your eyes or lower your gaze if this is more comfortable, allow your body to become limp as you allow the bed or couch beneath you to support your weight and begin with deep cleansing breaths.
Breathing in as deeply and fully as you can, filling the lungs and chest space on every inhale.

///

And as you exhale push the air out gradually, ensuring you empty the lungs in preparation for the next deep breath in.

And enjoy the relaxation that deep breathing provides, enjoy the sensation of breathing deeply and fully. Enjoy the experience of allowing your breath to relieve any tension in the muscles or any tightness in the limbs, all adding to your rapid weight loss.

And when you feel suitably relaxed you can allow your body to return to its natural pattern of breathing.

//

And as you lie here with your breath, this is a good time to see your personal speedboat in your imagination.

You may have sailed your own boat before or this may be your first time, just go ahead and create the image in your mind, the colour, the shape and the size.

///

And see yourself as a competent sailor, you have the ability and the know-how to sail your own boat, what a great way to relax and ease the body and the mind.

And now it's time to embark on your relaxing boat ride, sailing across the Caribbean sea in your very own small speedboat, to a secluded desert island, where you will be able to luxuriate in the privacy of a private beach hut without any interruption or disturbance.

///

And as you lay here, allow the music to guide you into deep relaxation. Let your thoughts dissolve into dreamy notions of the crystal blue seas that surround your green tropical island.

//

Let go of any tightness in the body that is holding onto the weight and gently breathe in the clean sea air, letting it cleanse and clear the cells of the body as you continue breathing out any tension or tightness.

/

And I'd like you to imagine now stepping into your speedboat and as you start the engine the gentle bubbling of the propeller in the water, gives you a sense of comfort and ease.

And as you take a hold of the rudder now you begin to guide your boat across the surface of the bluest clearest waters you have ever seen.

//

The sky above is light and airy with just a hint of blue, not a cloud to be seen just the occasional bird high up above as the ocean breeze caresses your body, keeping you cool and calm as you glide across the sea.

//

And as you begin to think about ways you can increase your weight loss through relaxation, start with one small area of your body where there is a little tension.

And just notice this area of tension at first.
Perhaps acknowledging how it got there.
Where it came from, and as you focus on this small spot of tightness, you can allow it to ease slightly, letting go of any excess weight, as you relax and repair the muscles, cells and limbs in the body.

///

And when you're ready to completely let go, take a deep breath in. And as you exhale drop the muscles and feel the full release.

//

And as you begin to slowly move through the water - check-in with yourself.
Noticing where you are tense,
holding or clenching in the body.

Check-in with the feet first,
noticing the ankles, and the toes.

Let them go.
Allow them to drop forward and wiggle the toes to make sure they are not gripping with tension.

///

And as you release the feet take a deep breath in if you need, to ensure you completely release them. Then take a look around at the open water.
The low waves gently lapping against the side of the boat are not too much or too little just enough to keep you moving gently across the sea.

///

And as you enjoy the beautiful turquoise waters, take another deep breath in and release the calves, perhaps clenching the muscles first for a count of 3 …1…2…3…and then releasing and relaxing the legs completely as you exhale.

///

Feel how heavy your legs are becoming now as you release the tension that you were holding onto. Knowing that the more you relax the faster the weight loss.

And as you listen to the water gently stirring all around you, allow the sounds of the ocean to soothe you and bring your awareness to the thighs and the knees.
Notice the position of your knees now, perhaps they are a little bent or completely straight. You can try shifting around to release any cramps or stiffness that you experience here.

///

And the salty scent of the sea is penetrating your senses now, reminding you of long walks on the beach. As you steer the boat, notice the rhythmic humming of the small engine vibrating in time with your breathing. Each breath brings in more relaxation and optimises your weight loss.

///

Allow yourself to shift from doing to being, noticing how easy it is to be carried along by the water, smoothly sailing towards the deserted beach in the distance.

///

Now arriving at the hips and pelvis area. Going deep into the muscles into the joints if necessary, checking for small spots of holding and breathing into them to release them.

///

It's time to relax, truly relax, letting go of the body, letting go of the mind and allowing every limb to fall now. Allowing the body to be limp and heavy. Allowing the weight to go.

///

There is nothing for you to do right now, but let go, relax and release, as you sail effortlessly across the turquoise seas of the Caribbean.

///

And bring your awareness to the lower back now, noticing the tension held in the spine or the lower abdomen, allowing them both to expand as you breathe in deeply. Pushing them all the way out and allowing them to release and collapse fully on the exhale.

Spend a few minutes relaxing the lower back and abdomen.

///

And when you feel the release you can move your awareness up towards the upper back and chest area, and again take a deep breath in.
With the gentle waves and sound of the water encouraging you, expand the upper back and chest all the way out, filling both with clean sea air.

Clearing any negative energy that has been hanging around, letting go of any emotions that cause weight retention and allowing your body to relax fully.

Refreshing the chest, lungs and upper back with the salty sea breeze that surrounds you now. Imagine all of the stress, anxiety and extra pounds leaving with the salty sea air, let it go, let it go, let it all go.

///

And as you take in the sea air, the sun warms your head, shoulders, neck and back, allowing you to relax them, dropping the shoulders, releasing the tension in your neck, as you gently turn it from side to side, perhaps dropping the head and tucking the chin slightly.

///

And as you look ahead towards the green island that beckons you to come closer, you notice flying fish jumping on the horizon, what a sight, how exciting and joyful they seem. How playful and fun they must be.

//

As you drop your gaze, you can see all the way down to the sea bed, covered in vibrant green plants, brightly coloured coral covered in fish, large and small of every colour and description. They dart in and out, energetically, while the occasional jellyfish, lazily drift around, relaxed and at ease.

///

Imagine breathing relaxation in with every clean fresh breath, and breathing any lingering tension and excess weight out.
Following the rhythm of the waves in the water with your breathing, allowing it to ease you into a deeper state of calm and tranquillity.

///

This is the life, getting closer and closer to the white sandy beach ahead.
Feeling more and more relaxed.
Calmer and calmer.
Breathing nice and easy, soft and slow.
Surrendering lower and lower, deeper and deeper to the sounds of the Caribbean sea.

///

And finally, as your boat arrives, easing onto the shoreline, you can relax the jaw, the muscles around the eyes and the forehead and release any tension that may have returned as you prepare to explore your very own private beach.

///

As you step out of the boat, wading through the water onto the beach, you feel optimistic about the good night's sleep that awaits you.
It's time to explore, this is your private island, there is nobody here to disturb you or interrupt your peace.

/

This is your private, secret place especially for you, the place where you can return whenever you need some peace and quiet, whenever you are in need of a good night's sleep.

//

And now as you walk across the warm sand, allowing the tiny grains to fall between your toes, you see a large, well-crafted beach hut, standing majestically on four stilts.
A welcoming silhouette against the horizon.

///

And as you wade through the sand, you can enjoy the beauty of the setting sun in the distance. The pink and orange giving everything around you a warm glow.

The warm early evening sunset conspires with the gentle lapping waves of the sea and the softly swaying palm trees to create the ideal atmosphere for a good night's sleep.

And as you push forward each step heavier than the last, taking you a little deeper into the sand, each time the sand holds your feet a little longer, each time your whole body sinking a little deeper and deeper as you get closer and closer.

And finally, as you drag your tired feet, your weary body swaying in the heat, you arrive.
It's time, It's time to rest, time to put your feet up as you enter your luxury beach hut.

///

And as you climb the small steps, and enter into the ambience of pure luxury, you see the large fan that rotates effortlessly hanging from the high slanting bamboo roof. You're grateful for the cool breeze that pushes away the humid heat throughout. The cool wooden floors beneath your feet varnished and glistening add to the cool temperature as you walk.

/

You spot a hammock hanging in the corner by an open window, this will be your bed for the night. And as you climb in, you lay your head back and allow the gentle sway of the hammock to ease your weary body.

///

In the last moments of wakefulness, you allow your eyelids to close, heavy from your journey and observe the willingness of your body to completely surrender. Your mind is soothed by the sounds of the ocean waves. It's time for sleep.

And as you ease into a state of slumber, there is nothing for you to do right now but enjoy the peace and tranquillity of your private desert island.

The sounds of the Caribbean Sea in the background, erasing the stress of the day.
As you willingly let all of the pressure and tension just melt away.

///

The fan continues to create a gentle steady breeze above.
Your hammock sways back and forth. Ever so gently, back and forth, back and forth.

///

Outside of the window now the palm trees and the waves are becoming quieter and quieter as the sun sets, barely audible as you drift off.

And as you let go, drifting off, the warmth of the sun melting away any fat cells and building your muscle mass, you fall into complete relaxation, you are at peace and nature is doing its work.

Feeling totally calm and utterly relaxed, tomorrow is another day.

Night, night, and sweet dreams.

Session 5: Affirmations - Overcoming Insomnia

Overview: This affirmation session is designed to reprogram one's unconscious mind to produce a deep, restful and healthy sleep every night.

Time: 30-minutes *[Repeat the affirmations 4 times for them to take effect in the mind of the listener.]*

[Reader Notes]

- Read the following script at a steady pace, taking your time to guide the listener with your voice.
- Allow long comfortable pauses, that you are happy with, in between passages and follow the key set out below to allow longer pauses.

[Pause Key]

... Very short pause: Reader pauses for 2 seconds

/ Short pause: Reader pauses for 10 seconds

// Medium pause: Reader pauses for 20 seconds

/// Long pause: Reader pauses for 30 seconds

[Script Begins]

Hello and welcome to this powerful affirmation session….

Affirmations are used to reprogram the unconscious beliefs and behaviours to sleep soundly and pleasantly all night.

Listening to this audio file on a daily basis can bring about tremendous positive changes.

These affirmations focus on good sleep hygiene, long-lasting healthy sleep, restful sleep and having good dreams. Listen to this audio daily for a minimum of 40 days for best results.

Relax, and enjoy!

I fall asleep easily when bedtime approaches
I sleep soundly
I sleep pleasantly
I am a deep sleeper
I am a sound sleeper
I sleep throughout the night until I wake up in the morning
I am a peaceful sleeper
I am a quiet sleeper
I am comfortable in bed
I am peaceful in bed
My mind is quiet when I am in bed
Going to sleep is easy for me
Falling asleep is easy
I sleep healthily and restfully
I sleep deeply every night
Each day as bedtime approaches I am calm
I am optimistic about falling asleep every night
Every night going to sleep is a pleasant experience
I have good dreams when I sleep
I have peaceful dreams when I sleep
My mind is silent as I fall asleep
I let go and drift into a deep sleep every night as soon as my head touches the pillow
My pillow is comfortable
My body relaxes easily and quickly when I am in bed
My mind relaxes easily and quickly when I am in bed
I let go of all unnecessary nervous tension as soon as I get into bed
I am undisturbed by light when I am asleep
I sleep easy every night
Every night sleeping is a pleasant experience
I look forward to sleeping every night
The harder I try to stay awake the drowsier I become
I start to become drowsier and drowsier as soon as I close my eyes in bed
As I close my eyes in bed my muscles begin to relax
My breathing becomes deep and calm as soon as I get into bed to fall asleep

I am positive about falling asleep easily every night
I sleep soundly all night and wake up pleasantly in the morning
I always have a restful sleep
I always have pleasant and good dreams
I am a happy sleeper
I am always energised after a good night's rest
I am relaxed when bedtime approaches
My mind and body are ready to rest in bed
Sleeping is a very natural state for me
Optimism and happy thoughts fill my dreams
I do my best to ensure my sleep environment is clean and comfortable
I choose sleep, rest, peace and relaxation
I am truly grateful that my body and mind rest easily every night
My sleep is healing
I undergo an emotional, mental and physical healing process every time I sleep
I am worthy of a good night's rest
I deserve to have a healthy restful sleep
I enjoy an undisturbed night of sleep every night

Session 6: Affirmations - Extreme fat burn

Overview: This affirmation session is designed to reprogram one's unconscious mind to burn fat faster.

Time: 30-minutes ***[Repeat the affirmations 4 times for them to take effect in the mind of the listener.]***

[Reader Notes]

- Read the following script at a steady pace, taking your time to guide the listener with your voice.
- Allow long comfortable pauses, that you are happy with, in between passages and follow the key set out below to allow longer pauses.

[Pause Key]

… Very short pause: Reader pauses for 2 seconds

/ Short pause: Reader pauses for 10 seconds

// Medium pause: Reader pauses for 20 seconds

/// Long pause: Reader pauses for 30 seconds

[Script Begins]

Hello and welcome to this powerful affirmation session….

These affirmations are used to reprogram the unconscious mind to start burning fat at a faster rate.

Listening to this audio file on a daily basis can bring about tremendous positive changes.

These affirmations focus on burning fat at a faster rate by exercising more regularly. Listen to this audio daily for a minimum of 40 days for best results.

Relax, and enjoy!

I am burning fat quicker every day
I am losing weight easily
I lose more weight every day
Fat is easy to burn
I am worthy of losing weight
I am worthy of being slim
I am worthy of exercising daily
I am happy that I exercise every day
I am excited to lose weight
Burning fat is easy
Losing weight is easy
I am motivated to exercise every day
I feel like exercising every day
My fat burns faster every time I exercise
I lose my excess fat quickly and easily
Burning fat comes naturally to me
Exercising is a natural part of my daily routine
I feel bad when I skip a day of exercise
I am grateful that I enjoy exercising daily
I am grateful that I am losing more and more weight rapidly each day
I am motivated to do what it takes to burn more fat each and every day
Each and everyday I am becoming thinner and thinner
I enjoy burning more fat each day
It makes me happy to see my weight reduce
I burn more fat as I sleep
Exercise accelerates my fat burning process
My metabolism is very high
My body is a fat burning furnace
My body converts fat to energy
My body efficiently burns stored fat
My weight decreases day by day
My body responds to exercise by shedding fat
The more fat I burn the better I feel
My body wants to return to a healthy weight
Every moment of the day I am burning fat
I love the feeling of having lower body fat
I choose health over excess body fat

I burn fat efficiently and effectively

I love physical fitness

Physical fitness makes me feel empowered and amazing

Fat melts off me easily

My metabolism is at its optimal rate and it burns fat quickly

I am a physically active person

Every day I am becoming slimmer and fitter

Exercising is empowering and exciting

Everytime I sweat I burn more calories

My body is burning calories faster each day

I am losing weight every single moment

I make sure that I exercise every day without fail

I deserve to lose weight

I deserve to burn more fat every day

I am free of all obstacles that are preventing me from losing weight

I am free of all the obstacles that prevent me from exercising

My body is healthily burning every excess pound

I look forward to burning fat every day

I look forward to exercising every day

I am truly grateful that my body and mind work diligently to burn off the excess fat on my body in a healthy and natural manner

Session 7: Affirmations - Overcoming Body Anxiety

Overview: This affirmation session is designed to reprogram one's unconscious mind to overcome body anxiety.

Time: 30-minutes ***[Repeat the affirmations 4 times for them to take effect in the mind of the listener.]***

[Reader Notes]

- Read the following script at a steady pace, taking your time to guide the listener with your voice.
- Allow long comfortable pauses, that you are happy with, in between passages and follow the key set out below to allow longer pauses.

[Pause Key]

… Very short pause: Reader pauses for 2 seconds

/ Short pause: Reader pauses for 10 seconds

// Medium pause: Reader pauses for 20 seconds

/// Long pause: Reader pauses for 30 seconds

[Script Begins]

Hello and welcome to this powerful affirmation session….

These affirmations are used to reprogram the unconscious mind to start loving and appreciating your body.

Listening to this audio file on a daily basis can bring about tremendous positive changes.

These affirmations focus on overcoming body anxiety by working on loving and appreciating your body. Listen to this audio daily for a minimum of 40 days for best results.

Relax, and enjoy!

I am beautiful
I love my body
I am becoming thinner and thinner
I enjoy looking at my body
I am comfortable in my own body
I am comfortable in my skin
I am grateful for my body
I am worthy of becoming my ideal weight
My body is beautiful
My inner beauty shines forth daily
Every day I give thanks for my body
I appreciate and give love to all parts of my body
I am pretty
I feel beautiful
I feel in love with my body
I give my body the attention that it requires
I give my body the care that it needs
I look after my body
Giving love to my body is important to me
Giving thanks to my body is important to me
I am proud of who I am
I love myself
I am confident about my body
I am confident about myself
I believe in myself
I believe I can transform my body
I enjoy giving thanks to my body
I praise my body
I am connected to my body
I am in sync with my body
I care deeply about the health of my body
I do my best to look after my body every day
I say loving things about my body

I think loving thoughts about my body

I am comfortable being in my body in public

I enjoy being appreciated

I enjoy being beautiful

I am thankful that I am beautiful

I am thankful that I feel beautiful

I am impressed with the progress of my body every day

I am thankful I work hard to improve my body

I am motivated to love my body more and more

I am motivated to transform my body

I work hard to ensure my body is healthy and loved

My love for my body is so strong that other people can feel it

I am so comfortable and confident within myself that other people compliment me

I compliment my body

I am comfortable being me

I am truly empowered to love and accept my body

I appreciate every part of my body

I am grateful that I accept my body fully and completely

I am perfect and complete just the way I am

My body is a vessel for my ultimate potential

Being whole and grounded makes me beautiful

I deserve to be treated with love and respect

I deserve to be beautiful

I deserve to be loved for who I am

I trust the wisdom of my body

My body is an amazing gift, I treat it with love and respect

Conclusion

Thank you for listening
Find more help @_____

Extreme Weight Loss Hypnosis: Positive Affirmations, Guided Meditations & Hypnotic Gastric Band For Rapid Fat Burn, Self-Love, Over thinking, Emotional Eating & Healthy Habits

by
Self-Healing Mindfulness Academy

© Copyright 2021 - All rights reserved.

The content contained within this book may not be reproduced, duplicated or transmitted without direct written permission from the author or the publisher.
Under no circumstances will any blame or legal responsibility be held against the publisher, or author, for any damages, reparation, or monetary loss due to the information contained within this book; either directly or indirectly.

Legal Notice:
This book is copyright protected. This book is only for personal use. You cannot amend, distribute, sell, use, quote or paraphrase any part, or the content within this book, without the consent of the author or publisher.

Disclaimer Notice:
Please note the information contained within this document is for educational and entertainment purposes only. All effort has been executed to present accurate, up to date, and reliable, complete information. No warranties of any kind are declared or implied. Readers acknowledge that the author is not engaging in the rendering of legal, financial, medical or professional advice.

This book contains a total of 12 guided meditations, affirmations, and hypnosis scripts to help you lose weight and achieve your ideal shape and size. The total running time for all the scripts combined will be 10 hours. Proper instructions have been included for the narrator regarding when to pause and resume the narration.

The scripts are in the following order:

I. Three simple tips to help you lose weight..4

II. Weight Loss Meditations...6

   2. Shedding the extra weight (45 minutes) 11

   3. Visualization for Weight Loss (50 minutes)... 18

   4. Lose Weight effortlessly (60 minutes) 25

III. Quit Smoking Affirmations 32

   5. Affirmations for Healthy Eating Habits (40 minutes)................................. 32

   6. Affirmations for Rapid Weight loss (60 minutes) 42

IV. Quit Smoking Hypnosis 52

   7. Weight Loss Hypnosis – I (40 minutes) 52

   8. Weight loss Hypnosis – II (45 minutes) 58

   9. Weight Loss Hypnosis – III (50 minutes)... 65

   10. Weight Loss Hypnosis – IV (60 minutes) 71

   11. Weight Loss Hypnosis (Before Sleep) – I (60 minutes).............................. 78

   12. Weight Loss Hypnosis (Before Sleep) – II (60 minutes) 86

I. Three simple tips to help you lose weight

The journey to weight loss is never easy, don't you agree? From following a strict diet plan to trying out rigorous exercise regimes, so much sweat and patience go into it. And even after initial success, maintaining that level of discipline becomes difficult and all the progress that you made begins to fade away. And soon you find yourself back to square one. And you say to yourself, "Damn! I am never gonna lose weight." But this isn't true. Just because it seems hard doesn't mean you can't get there. After all, there can't be only one way to achieve success. And success is not always directly proportional to the amount of sacrifice you do. Sometimes, change comes by making a simple tweak in how you do your routine activities. By modifying your habits a bit, you can bring a drastic change in how you approach your weight loss goal. And that's what I am going to talk about in this chapter. So, here are three simple tips that you must imbibe in your life to reach your ideal weight and size more quickly and easily.

1. Eat mindfully

I want you to pause and think about this for a moment – how often do you think about the process of eating while you are actually eating? If the answer is "never", you now know where the problem lies. When we are eating food (even our most favourite ones) our mind is always thinking about random stuff. We simply don't enjoy the act of eating. It's quite an irony that we think about food all the time except when we are actually eating.
So, here's what I want you to do – whenever you sit to eat, be fully conscious of the act of eating. And I don't mean just chewing the food properly but the entire act of eating. So, the next time you have food in front of you on your table, be present. Acknowledge the food: see the food as the source of nourishment and nutrition and as a fuel for your body. Bring in all your senses. Hold the food item in your hand, feel the texture, look at it consciously, smell the aroma. And when you take a bite, feel the texture, the taste; feel it melting inside your mouth; chew the food at least twenty times. Be aware of the chewing, the swallowing and then pausing between each bite. You may even put down your fork and knife and taking a mindful breath before taking the next bite. Eat each bite thoroughly; take the time to taste the food. Enjoy the process, really savour each bite. Each bite should be magical. And you will notice how much your meal tastes better now when you consume it mindfully.

2. Differentiate physical hunger from emotional hunger

You must try to understand the difference between the true physical hunger and the false emotional hunger. Physical hunger is when you are actually hungry and it starts slowly and grows slowly. The emotional hunger, on the other hand, is because of a change in your state of mind and comes almost immediately. The physical hunger can be held back for a while is easily satisfied with nutritious and healthy food. Whereas the emotional hunger demands urgent satisfaction and too usually with specific unhealthy food items like chocolates, junk food, etc.

Once you learn to differentiate your emotional hunger from your physical hunger, you can manage your diet intake in a much controlled way. Being able to recognise the signs of emotional hunger helps you deal with your emotional eating habits. And you will learn how to manage your emotional changes without using food as a means to do so. Always remember, food is to nourish and energise you, not to a means to cope with stress or emotional issues. So, whenever you feel hungry, ask yourself if the hunger is physical or emotional.

3. Listen to your stomach

Your stomach gives you a signal every time you are satiated. But you are so engrossed in the act of unmindful eating that you miss that signal and continue to stuff your mouth with more food. And this obviously results in weight gain. The key is to eat slowly and listen to the signal of the stomach. If you ignore the signal, you will continue to eat whatever is left on your plate and not just that you may even refill your plate because you are not sure if you are already full. That's what we need to avoid.

Always eat in smaller sized plates because it prevents you from overloading the food. You know you can always refill. Eat mindfully and slowly. The moment you feel that you are satiated, just stop. Eat only as much as your stomach needs. If you feel hungry after a short while, go and eat again. You don't need to starve yourself. But every time you put sit to eat, listen to the alarm in your stomach. And when your stomach says, "That's it, I am full", stop right there. Listen to the signals of your stomach and you may see the health rewards coming your way.

II. Weight Loss Meditations

1. The ideal self image (30 minutes)

Meditation is a wonderful tool to help you achieve any goal, including your goal to lose weight. How? Because when you are in the state of deep meditation, your life source energy comes in close contact the ultimate source. And when, at this level of connection, you put in a prayer or affirmation or you sincerely visualize your goal, the whole universe conspires to turn that intention into reality. That's why while practicing the meditations in this series your intentions will be of utmost importance.

[5 seconds pause]

Now, in a short while I will be guiding you into a meditative state of deep healing and relaxation to help you achieve your goal of weight loss. You can choose a comfortable spot to sit and relax. Or you can choose to lie down if you like. When you are ready, close your eyes and pay attention to what I say. Deep healing becomes more effective when you are relaxed and ready to receive the positive vibes.

Now take a few deep breaths – in through your nose and out through the mouth. Breathe as deeply as you comfortably can. Do not be too hard but try to go as deep as possible. Remember to breathe in through the nose and out through the mouth.

[5 seconds pause]

Very nice! Continue to take deep breaths. In through the nose and out through the mouth.

[5 seconds pause]

In through the nose and out through the mouth.

[5 seconds pause]

In through the nose and out through the mouth.

[5 seconds pause]

In through the nose and out through the mouth.

[5 seconds pause]

In through the nose and out through the mouth.

And relax. Now breathe at your natural, relaxed pace.

[5 seconds pause]

 You are relaxed. You are at peace. You are relaxed. You are at peace. You are relaxed. You are at peace.

Now when you breathe in say it in your mind, "I am relaxed."

And when you breathe out, repeat, "I am at peace"

[5 seconds pause]
Breathe in, "I am relaxed." Breathe out, "I am at peace."
[5 seconds pause]
Breathe in, "I am relaxed." Breathe out, "I am at peace."
[5 seconds pause]
Breathe in, "I am relaxed." Breathe out, "I am at peace."
Breathe in relaxation. Breathe out peace.
[5 seconds pause]
Breathe in relaxation. Breathe out peace.
[5 seconds pause]
Breathe in relaxation. Breathe out peace.
[5 seconds pause]
Very nice; keep breathing this way.
[20 seconds pause]
Use your breath as an anchor to ground yourself into your body. Starting at the top of your head, begin to scan your body relaxing any unnecessary tension in your face and neck.
[5 seconds pause]
Now bring your awareness to your shoulders, now your chest, and your upper back, down to your lower back.
[5 seconds pause]
Feel tension melting away from all areas of your body. Let yourself be guided by the sensations you feel. Do not put a self-made reason or story to any sensation. Just allow yourself to experience awareness of your body, feel your organs, feel your normal areas of discomfort.
[5 seconds pause]
And if your mind wanders into its own world of thoughts, gently bring it back to this body scan. Find new areas of discomfort.
[5 seconds pause]
Is there a part of your body that requires more attention? Breath into these areas, feel all the extra space within your body that you have created and filled with goodness. Moving through your body feel your awareness, what it is like to be fully present with sensation of your body?
[5 seconds pause]
And if your mind wanders into its own world of thoughts, gently bring it back to this body scan.
[5 seconds pause]

Now direct your awareness to your feet and ankles. Feel the top of your feet beside of your feet's bottom feet .and then shifting your awareness to the legs, the front, the sides and the back of your legs. All the way up to your hips.

[5 seconds pause]

Now choose to shift your awareness to your belly. Your sides, and then over to your lower back; breathing up to your mid back and your upper back.

[5 seconds pause]

Now Guide yourself to your shoulders; around your neck, down to your chest and all the way down to your arms and hands and your wrist, and into your fingertips.

[5 seconds pause]

Feel the sensations completely without any reason. And begin to feel sensation and awareness to your neck. And up to your head. Feel your face, your mouth, your jaw line, and your cheek bones.

[5 seconds pause]

Feel your nose, feel your eyes, feel your eyebrows and your forehead. Choose to shift your awareness to your hair and the top of your head.

[5 seconds pause]

Feel your breath once again. Feel your body completely relaxed, happy and healthy. Feel the full presence of you in your entire body as a whole.

[5 seconds pause]

Feel that your body is now relaxed, completely at ease. All the cells, muscles, and joints in your body are completely relaxed. Feel a sense of calmness and peace in every nook and corner of your body, relaxing you completely.

[1 minute pause]

Now I want you to visualize yourself at your ideal self. Create in your mind a picture about how you would look when you are at your perfect weight and ideal shape and size. I want you to be as vivid and clear as possible. You are at your fittest, wearing the finest clothes showcasing your tones physique, your skin glowing and radiating, your eyes brimming with confidence. Make sure the mental image is clear, crisp, and bright. Look at all the details – your hair, your nails, your skin – everything about you is glowing with health. Look how slim you are – your perfect tummy, your arms and legs and shoulders – as perfect as they could be. See this perfect looking you standing in front of you. Look at the confidence that comes with such great health and fitness. The charisma is unmatchable.

[5 seconds pause]

Now float into that perfect self. Be at your ideal shape and size. Feel the confidence, feel the charisma that is your own. Look from the eyes of the perfect you, listen from the ears. Feel the feeling. You are in control. You know that this perfect body and size did not come easy. You had to really sweat it out. But now that have achieved this level of fitness, you are going to keep it maintain it. And you feel so proud about yourself. After all, it was your own hard work that paid off. You made a decision to lose weight, you decided to regularly exercise, you decided to give your one hundred percent to your fitness, and the results are in front of you – a perfect looking you at your ideal weight, looking exactly how you have always wanted to look.

[5 seconds pause]

And you go into the flashback of how you attained this level of fitness and health. And you see yourself in sweating it out in your favorite way – whether it's going for a run, cycling, swimming, playing a sport or hitting the gym. Or you could mix multiple regimes. It's all up to you. And you see yourself twisting your body, you can see the sweat all your skin after a training and fitness session. And after the session, you feel so energetic and fresh. You take a shower and start your day. And you realize how productive and efficient you are becoming on work front. And when it's meal time, you choose your food wisely, eating only the healthy and nutrient rich food. After such a good exercise session, the sight of unhealthy sugar-coated or deeply fried items makes you feel disgusted. You go for fresh fruits and veggies. You drink a lot of water to keep yourself hydrated. And you notice how tasty this healthy and nutrient-rich food feels now.

[5 seconds pause]

And after a productive day, you go to bed and your tired body dozes off instantly. And next morning, you wake up completely reinvigorated and refreshed. And you are ready to start again. And you see how quickly your hard work is paying off with superb results. Day after day, you work out hard, you eat healthy food, and you take good rest – and the results are there just in front of you. Boom – you are at your ideal weight, shape, and size. It was your hard work that paid off. You now feel so proud of your body.

[5 seconds pause]

Visualize yourself at your ideal shape and size as vividly as possible. Look how good your body is now. You are looking just perfect – exactly how you always wanted to be. This is real. What we can feel with full conviction we can definitely achieve it too. So feel that feeling of being at your best body ever. Look at your perfect self as clearly and as vividly as possible. Look at all the minute details; see how much progress you have made. This is how you have always wanted to look and now you are looking at that perfect, ideal self image of you.

[2 minutes pause]

Take three deep breaths and release yourself from all fears and doubts. The time for change has come. All you need to do is be ready for it.

[20 seconds pause]

Now I will be counting from one to ten and with each number, feel the commitment to reach your ideal self multiplying within you. Feel the feeling and be one with it. Soak in the image of your ideal self. So, we start now.

[5 seconds pause]

One: Step into the picture of that ideal self that you created in this meditation.

Two: Become the person in that picture.

Three: Feel the feeling. How good does it feel now to be at your ideal weight and size?

Four: See from the eyes of that slimmer you with a perfect body.

Five: You feel so strong and confident.

Six: You feel the changes in your personality.

Seven: You feel happier and fulfilled

Eight: You know how much this means to you.

Nine: You make the commitment to maintain this body.

Ten: Be the person in that image. You are now that person with the ideal body.

[20 seconds pause]

Store that image and that feeling in your heart chakra, located in the centre of your chest.

[10 seconds pause]

Raise your left hand and place it on your chest centre. Now raise your right hand and place it on your left hand. Calm yourself down. Feel the rise and fall of your chest. Listen to the beating of your heart. Know that what you just experienced is reality that is about to happen. Keep this image and this feeling in your heart chakra throughout your weight loss journey. Great progress is just around the corner.

[10 seconds pause]

You can now bring your hands to your eyes and gently massage them.

[5 seconds pause]

And when you are ready, gently open your eyes and come back.

2. Shedding the extra weight (45 minutes)

You are listening to this audio because you want to lose weight. Shedding the extra weight is not just about looking better; it's much more than that. It's about your self-esteem, your confidence, and your energy levels. Being at your ideal weight gives you the strength and the stamina to be better and more efficient at work. It gives you an edge when you socialize. It makes you feel more in control over your life.
[5 seconds pause]
So, adjust yourself into a posture of comfort that will keep you aware for the duration of this session. And when you are ready, gently close your eyes.
[5 seconds pause]
Now take a deep breath in through your nose. Hold it for a moment. And then release from the mouth fully emptying your lungs.
[5 seconds pause]
Take another deep breath in through your nose. Hold. And exhale from the mouth.
[5 seconds pause]
Take one more breath this way.
[5 seconds pause]
Now relax. Breathe at your natural pace.
[20 seconds pause]
If your mind wanders, gently bring it back. Be here in the present moment. Be fully alive in this moment – the here, the now.
[5 seconds pause]
You are here in the present moment. Feel your energies resonating within you. Feel the flow of energy in your body.
[5 seconds pause]
Now begin to feel into your body. Start with your head; and as you feel and sense your head, see or feel a healing pink light entering your body. Let it fill your mind, your facial muscles, your skull, and your ears.
[5 seconds pause]
Now let it travel down to your neck, your shoulders.
[5 seconds pause]
This is the pink healing light that has the power to heal you as you relax, let go. Let this pink healing light releases from you all burdens as you relaxes your shoulders and the sense down into your chest.

[5 seconds pause]
Now feel it in your shoulder blades and upper back. And this pink healing light fills your heart and lungs, your stomach, all organs in your body.
[5 seconds pause]
Now feel the energy spreading into your torso and your middle back and travel down to your hips. And feel it entering your vertebrae, every vertebra in your spine is filled with pink light and it enters your blood stream; filling your blood with light.
[5 seconds pause]
Now it travels down into your legs and your feet. It travels through your veins, your cardio vascular system. Now this pink surrounds you. It is now healing your skin. Allow yourself to bath now in this pink healing light.
[20 seconds pause]
Relax. Relax. Relax
[5 seconds pause]
What did you feel? Did you feel any sensations in your body? Did you sense any change in energy levels?
[5 seconds pause]
Let's bring your awareness back to your body now and try to feel the sensations.
[5 seconds pause]
Scan your body starting with the base of your feet. Can you sense your toes? Soften your toes and spread that softness to the ankle.
[5 seconds pause]
Now scan your lower leg and the knee on the right and the knee on the left.
[5 seconds pause]
Feel the release of any pent up tension in those areas. And then you bring your awareness to your thigh bones and your pelvis. Release the tension.
[5 seconds pause]
And if your mind wanders into its own world of thoughts, gently bring it back to this body scan. Take a deep breath in… and breathe out.
[5 seconds pause]
Take another deep breath in… and out.
[5 seconds pause]
And one more time – a deep breath in… and out.
[5 seconds pause]
Now bring your awareness to your ankles, shin bones or the knees, and release any stress that may be holding there.
[5 seconds pause]

Now moving up and scanning your hips, releasing the stress. Now scan the navel center, the lower back, the abdominal region. So you send your softness, your breath and your ability to let things be so just so. As you scan the body up by the external parts feeling even more so the pressure changes in your body.

[5 seconds pause]

Continuing scanning your body and letting your shoulders, your arms, wrist and hands, feel heavy in the bones, to reveal that lightness that is in the body. You may feel that there is resistance in throat where the back of the neck.

[5 seconds pause]

And even here we just trend with the breaths. Sometimes gently soft swallow and filling up with that nostril breathing will rinse even more. Unclench the jaw, sense of slack, in the face, to the tongue and the eyes.

[5 seconds pause]

Scan the forehead and the scalp; release the stress from there as well. If thoughts are appearing just noticing that the thoughts are appearing and coming back to that the feeling of practicing, presence, moving the breath through as a way of bouncing what you are holding on to and what you are letting go off. To take refuge in this practice as we scan our body. Giving more allowance inside for spaciousness, for patience and that feeling of soaking in your breath and tuning into your body.

[5 seconds pause]

Take a deep breath in… and breathe out.

[5 seconds pause]

Take another deep breath in… and out.

[5 seconds pause]

And one more time – a deep breath in… and out.

[5 seconds pause]

Keep a gentle awareness on the flow of your breath – the inflow and the outflow.

[20 seconds pause]

And as you breathe at your normal pace, let's shift our focus towards your goal of weight loss. Meditation is a wonderful tool achieve that goal because when you in the state of meditation, you are connected with the ultimate source. And when at this level of connection, you put in a prayer or affirmation or visualize your goal; the whole universe conspires to turn that intention into reality.

[5 seconds pause]

Your body has innate intelligence. It already knows what the ideal weight is and how to get to this weight. Continue to breathe and relax. Today we are going to release the blocks that prevent you from allowing your body to transition into its perfect weight. Extra weight brings with it extra burden of diseases, stress and a feeling in insecurity. Having said that you must bear in mind that being overweight is not your fault. If you eat more than you should, there must be many underlying reasons for it. It may be that you use food as a defense mechanism to cope with stress and anxiety. Maybe you find it difficult to differentiate emotional hunger from physical hunger. All these are not your faults. Your subconscious mind has been wired in such a way that you turn to food to manage your stress or out of sheer habit. Today, we are going to work on your subconscious mind to change these habits.

[5 seconds pause]

To make a start, tap into your awareness of the present moment. Be in the here in the now. Notice your breathing – notice the inhale, notice the exhale.

[5 seconds pause]

Notice the inhale, notice the exhale.

[5 seconds pause]

Notice the inhale, notice the exhale.

[5 seconds pause]

Now repeat after me, "I am willing to release mu old habits and patterns that no longer serve me. I am willing to change the way I see food. I am willing to make changes to my lifestyle to help my body achieve its perfect weight."

[5 seconds pause]

Very nice; did you feel anything? Did you sense any changes inside of you? Even if you didn't it's completely fine.

Let's do this one more time and this time with more conviction and belief, "I am willing to release mu old habits and patterns that no longer serve me. I am willing to change the way I see food. I am willing to make changes to my lifestyle to help my body achieve its perfect weight."

[5 seconds pause]

That was really good. Now to make sure that the message seeps deep into you, we are going to repeat it the third time. This time, bring your entire focus on the words and their meaning. "I am willing to release mu old habits and patterns that no longer serve me. I am willing to change the way I see food. I am willing to make changes to my lifestyle to help my body achieve its perfect weight."

[5 seconds pause]

Connect with the feeling. Very nice; I want you to stay in this state for a while to let the healing take its course.

[30 seconds pause]

If you find that your mind has wandered, gently bring it back. What we just did with the affirmations was just the beginning. It's time to go a step further now. We need to release the mental blocks that hinder your progress. You might have noticed that just when your weight loss efforts begin to show result, your momentum takes a hit and you find yourself back to the place from where you started. That's because of your blocked subconscious mind. You have unintentionally created so many mental blocks that success on weight front continues to elude you. That's why it is important to remove those blocks as well.

Begin by deepening your breath. Notice your breathing – notice the inhale, notice the exhale.

[5 seconds pause]

Notice the inhale, notice the exhale.

[5 seconds pause]

Notice the inhale, notice the exhale.

[5 seconds pause]

Now repeat with me the following affirmations. "I let go of my fears and doubts about weight loss. I know that I am meant to be fit, healthy, and toned, and I remove any blockages that have been preventing me from achieving that state. I heal my emotions and feelings and make substantial progress on my journey to my ideal weight and size."

[5 seconds pause]

Very nice; did you feel anything? Did you sense any changes inside of you? Even if you didn't it's completely fine.

Let's do this one more time and this time with more conviction and belief, "I let go of my fears and doubts about weight loss. I know that I am meant to be fit, healthy, and toned, and I remove any blockages that have been preventing me from achieving that state. I heal my emotions and feelings and make substantial progress on my journey to my ideal weight and size."

[5 seconds pause]

That was really good. Now to make sure that the message seeps deep into you, we are going to repeat it the third time. This time, bring your entire focus on the words and their meaning. "I let go of my fears and doubts about weight loss. I know that I am meant to be fit, healthy, and toned, and I remove any blockages that have been preventing me from achieving that state. I heal my emotions and feelings and make substantial progress on my journey to my ideal weight and size."

[5 seconds pause]

Connect with the feeling. Very nice; I want you to stay in this state for a while to let the healing take its course.

[30 seconds pause]

Come back to the present moment. The road to lose weight isn't simply about body control. It's so much more to do with mind control.

[5 seconds pause]

So, stay relaxed while I command your subconscious mind. You need not worry about anything. You need not worry if you are not properly attentive or if you are feeling sleepy. Even if you were asleep during the course of this meditation, your subconscious mind was attentive all the while. Your subconscious mind took note of the expectations you have about your weight loss. It was alert when you said the affirmations to remove the blockages to your weight loss journey.

[5 seconds pause]

So, simply relax and maintain a gentle focus on your breathing.

[5 seconds pause]

Notice your breathing – notice the inhale, notice the exhale.

[5 seconds pause]

Notice the inhale, notice the exhale.

[5 seconds pause]

Notice the inhale, notice the exhale.

[5 seconds pause]

Release all judgments and pre-decided notions that you have about weight loss. From now on, you will lose weight quickly and you will lose weight naturally. You will stop the self-hate and self-criticism that you have been inflicting upon yourself. You will not be ashamed of your body. The more you feel ashamed of your body, the more resistance you create for change. You will generate only positive emotions and feelings about your health and weight.

[5 seconds pause]

You will, from now on, be more alert and conscious all the time. This awareness will also positively affect your food intake habits. From now on, you will eat more consciously, eating each bite mindfully and with full awareness. You will chew eat bite properly before swallowing it. You will increase your water intake.

[5 seconds pause]

Your subconscious mind knows which food to eat and which to avoid. So, the next time you see junk food or oily or sugar-coated food items, your subconscious mind will generate feeling of disgust and you will turn away from those unhealthy foods. You will eat only fresh and healthy foods from now on.

[5 seconds pause]

Your subconscious mind will nudge you to exercise more often. So, you will now listen to your intuition and choose a form of activity that will be most beneficial to you. You will be targeting your weight loss goal from all corners. Your subconscious mind is finding ways to achieve those goals in the most effective of ways. And soon, you will find yourself at your ideal weight and size. For that, you know you have to listen to your intuition when it comes to food and exercise regimes. Your gut feeling will guide you to the path to weight loss. Listen carefully!

[5 seconds pause]

It's now time to come back to your awareness. I will be counting very slowly from five to zero. You also need not hurry. Follow my instructions as I guide you back home. You will be becoming more aware with each receding number, and become fully aware when I reach the number zero.

Five: You are here in the present moment now. Be in the here. Be in the now. Bring your consciousness back to your body. Slowly begin to realize that you are in your physical body. Slowly and gently come back to the present moment.

Four: Feel your body. Feel your feet, your legs, and your hips. Feel your abdomen and your chest region. Feel your entire spinal column, feel your back. Be aware of your hands and wrists and your elbows and your entire arms. Now your shoulders and neck and chin. Now bring your awareness into your entire face. Feel your eyes resting in your sockets; now your forehead and your scalp. In a moment, be aware of your entire physical body.

Three: Clench your fists. And release. Move your fingers and toes. Loosen up your shoulders. Rotate your ankles, knees. Relax your jaw.

Two: Feel the flow of energy. Be in the present moment. Feel your breath. Feel the sensations.

One: Be aware of the surroundings. Can you hear any sound coming from outside the room? Can you smell anything? Can you feel the textures of your clothing?

Zero: When you are ready, gently open your eyes. Welcome back!

3. Visualization for Weight Loss (50 minutes)

Before we begin, make sure you would not be disturbed for the duration of this meditation. Find a nice and quiet spot. Sit in an upright position. Bring your eyes to a gentle close. Relax. Take three cleansing breaths – in through your nose and out through your mouth. Breathe in as deeply as you can and breathe out fully, emptying your lungs.
[15 seconds pause]
Relax. Loosen up your body. Relax your jaw, relax your shoulders, relax your facial muscles.
[5 seconds pause]
Now bring your awareness to your body. Listen to your heartbeat.
[5 seconds pause]
Feel your chest gently rises and falls as you breathe.
[5 seconds pause]
Very nice; maintain a focus on your breathing – notice the in-breath, notice the out-breath.
[15 seconds pause]
Before you get deeper into this weight loss meditation, you need to understand a few things. To change you must first accept who you are. You must first see yourself as you are right now. You must embrace reality. To move forward you must first let go of the past.
Now repeat after me, "I accept myself as who I am." "I release the past and step towards a beautiful future." "I free myself of my own psychological barriers" "I forgive myself for the self-criticism and self-self-harm I did to myself." I love my body and wish to improve it."
[5 seconds pause]
Take three cleansing breaths – in through your nose and out through your mouth. Breathe in as deeply as you can and breathe out fully, emptying your lungs.
[15 seconds pause]
The cells in our body have the intelligence of their own. When we have negative thoughts about our body, these emotions get stored in our cells. That is why before we move any further, it is important to let go of any traumas of the past your body might be holding on to. So, repeat the affirmations one more time, with more conviction. "I accept myself as who I am." "I release the past and step towards a beautiful future." "I free myself of my own psychological barriers" "I forgive myself for the self-criticism and self-self-harm I did to myself." I love my body and wish to improve it."

[5 seconds pause]

Take three cleansing breaths – in through your nose and out through your mouth. Breathe in as deeply as you can and breathe out fully, emptying your lungs.

[15 seconds pause]

Focus on your breath. And really watch your breath. Just feel it notice everything about it as you breathe in and breathe out. Feel the sensations as you breathe in and you breathe out.

[5 seconds pause]

Notice any change in sensations as you breathe and you breathe out. Just watch the tiny details of your breaths.

[5 seconds pause]

Then start to lengthen your breath. Breathe longer, slower deeper breaths into your tummy, deep down into your abdomen. Fill your chest and your lungs, really fill your tummy and when you breathe out release all of that stagnant energy.

[5 seconds pause]

In every exhalation, breath out every bit of old stagnant oxygen, squeeze it out. And breathe in a new energy of the cleansing breath. Just do that for a few more breaths.

[15 seconds pause]

Now focus to breathe into your head space. So when you breathe, just focus on your head breath filling your head, face and as it fills your head and face imagine that your breath is starting to touch all the little muscles. Starting with your scalp and as the breath touches everything it starts to relax it. Enjoy the body scan as you release any stress stored in your body and mind. So focus on the top of your scalp and imagine that all of the hair follicles are softening and relaxing.

[5 seconds pause]

The back of your head, let go and completely relax. The space around your eyes softens and your eyes can roll up and relax slightly. Imagine that you are just staring into that space, endless space in the middle of your forehead. Allow your eyes to relax just into that. Enjoy the body scan as you release any stress stored in your body and mind. Your temples, your forehead, your cheeks all relax. Relax your jaw, move to the tongue to the roof of the mouth to your tongue to fully relax. Start to breathe into your neck and the back of your shoulder.

[5 seconds pause]

Focus on your breathing so that every time you breathe out, you release any tension you holding in your neck and shoulders. Start to let the muscles get soft and heavy.

[5 seconds pause]

Physically move your shoulder away. Pull them down away from your ears, let them get completely heavy. Just relax your shoulders.
[5 seconds pause]
When you breathe in imagine your breath relaxation itself. When you breathe out, you let go of tension and stress or worries, you let go of anything in your mind or your body that isn't serve you. Your breath, you're out breath is pleased, cleansing, just by breathing in and breathing out cleansing your body. Relax in it.
[5 seconds pause]
Allow your chest to soften. Allow to relax. Imagine the relaxation rolling down over your shoulders, down into your arms, down your arms to your elbows. From your elbows all the way down to your fingertips so your arms are quiet and still and relaxed. Enjoy the body scan as you release any stress stored in your body and mind
[5 seconds pause]
Let your lungs start to slow down, let your breaths becomes effortless and shallow. Let your whole body starting to just disappear into another time or place. And all is there is your conscious mind. Focus on your breath, relaxing your body.
[5 seconds pause]
Let your tummy soften and relax. Breathe deep into that space, hold so much emotion there. Enjoy the body scan as you release any stress stored in your body and mind. Let the muscle soften, let your digestive system slow down and just be at peace. Breathe, relax.
[5 seconds pause]
Relax your hips, your thighs, your knees. Your calf muscles are softened and relax. Your ankles, deep, deep relaxation vibrating throughout your entire being. All the way down to your toes.
[5 seconds pause]
Every part of your body from the top of your head to the tips of your toes is feeling comfortable and safe. Everything is relaxed and calm just by closing your eyes. Let your whole body go, just let go. Let your whole physical body disappear into complete relaxation. You are completely relaxed. Now bask in this relaxation for a while.
[10 minutes pause]
Now bring your awareness back to the present moment, back to the now.
[5 seconds pause]
Breathe in. Breathe out.
[5 seconds pause]
Breathe in. Breathe out
[5 seconds pause]
Breathe in. Breathe out.

[5 seconds pause]
Breathe in. Breathe out
[5 seconds pause]
Relax. Now say these affirmations, "I take full responsibility for this current state of my body. I built this body with my food choice and exercise routine. I am aware of everything that I put into this body. I realize that I am the maker of this physical health. I pledge to improve my health now. I pledge to take strong actions to get into better shape and size. I pledge to take the necessary efforts to reach my ideal body and health. "
[5 seconds pause]
Breathe in. Breathe out.
[5 seconds pause]
Breathe in. Breathe out
[5 seconds pause]
Breathe in. Breathe out.
[5 seconds pause]
Breathe in. Breathe out
[5 seconds pause]
Begin to imagine yourself walking down a wonderful path and a ground a soft with sand, grains that feel like the massage underneath your feet. The sand is warm and relaxing and there is a grassy parameter on the outside of this path that you are walking down. And on both side of you, there is an abundance of apple trees, orange trees, there is an abundance of vegetation and fruits all around you. And you are enchanted by the beauty of the sight.
[5 seconds pause]
The day is bright and sunny. And the sun's temperature is perfectly warm, bringing warmness to your skin.
[5 seconds pause]
Keep walking down this path and notice all the abundance around you. Notice the incredible greenery. Every breath you breathe in is fresh, coming from a life all around you.
[5 seconds pause]
Begin to have a child like sense of amazement and amusement upwards the earth provide us. Begin to see all kinds of vegetation growing, edible vegetation. Everything you can imagine is growing in this massive garden. And as you walk appreciate mother earth provides to us and now after the right there is an orange tree, walk over that orange tree. Step back and be present in this moment. Find one perfectly delicious and take it off of its stem off its branch. And take it with you, walk over now to the apple tree and grab apple

for you journey too and you have a nice bag resting on your shoulder, you can fit all of these wonderful, sweet, nourishing and delicious fruits.

[5 seconds pause]

Just beyond this apple tree there is a berry field, go ahead and put some strawberries in your bag as well. And there is blueberry next to it. Grab a handful of those delicious blueberries. Put them in a safe little pouch. It is such a beautiful sight. Now there are peaches just beyond the blueberries. Grab the pears and some grapes and put all of this into your bag. This bag has a magical quality too and it doesn't feel heavy at all. It feels light and abundant. It feels so calm and relaxing. Once you have gathered all the fruit go ahead and come back on to the warm sandy path. As you walk now look into your bag and pick out any of those fruits that we just collected.

[5 seconds pause]

And begin eating these delicious fruits and continue to walk. You can notice the taste and the texture of whatever you have decided to eat. Notice everything you can about its flavors. And begin to just feel in your body where this fruit goes with in the body energetically; it goes beyond the stomach, goes in the different parts of the body for healing, for restoration, for rejuvenation.

[5 seconds pause]

Breathing deeply and continuing to notice the scenery vast, open as the fields of garden fruits trees, vegetables, amazement this earth provides. You feel so blessed to be here. And at the very end for this walk, at the distance there is a table where incredible meal made of completely fresh vegetables. You feel so relaxed, so happy. And as if one of the most luxurious places in the world with most exquisite chefs making great meals, dressing from the earth , vinegars, oils natural herb, natural spices, everything is organic. Step back and be present in this moment. Everything has a beautiful glow to it and you sit down and you notice the food, you do not eat it yet. Notice the glow of this beautifully healthy food. You are enjoying every bit of it.

[5 seconds pause]

Allow yourself to have a moment of gratitude for the earth's natural ability to provide more than enough of everything we need. Step back and be present in this moment. And allow that gratitude to move you, feel it appreciate it. Then begin to eat this food. It's only vegetables, only fruits only organic. Everything has come from this garden. It has the best flavors you ever had.

[5 seconds pause]

Continue to breathe deeply and enjoy every bite. Eat calmly, patiently aware of every bite, not rushing but enjoying every bite. Before you even pick up your utensil, you finish the bite first; enjoy all of it flavors mixing together. Be present. Appreciate the healing entering your body. Before you pick up your utensil and now you have another bite. Eat slowly and mindfully.

[5 seconds pause]

Notice the view around you. The beautiful garden, lush greenery, the bright sun with a little bit of clouds cover. Just enough to offer some shade time to time. And take in a moment as if divinity is looking and smiling at you from all around. Now you notice yourself feeling full and you finish that last bite. Placing the utensils down, grabbing the napkin, cleaning your face; thanking the universe for this meal.

[5 seconds pause]

Allow yourself to stop right there with the strong sense of will and control. Do not need to consume any more. You are satiated, you are content, you are satisfied.

[5 seconds pause]

Now pick up, your bag, leaving the left over there it is not a waste. There will be another purpose for this food; whether for somebody else or for some animals. There is an abundance that all that we need. We have more than enough. Continue to walk away from the meal from the food.

[5 seconds pause]

Now look back and appreciate its nourishment and deliciousness. Know that the delicious experience welcome again but for now experiencing the other side of feeling completely satisfied and contend. And begin to walk forward. Notice that you have become so energetic, healthy, and appreciative of this healthy body. Continue walking forward.

[5 seconds pause]

Notice whatever beautiful scenery in front of you and find a nice cozy spot to sit down and look up at the sky and allowing yourself to just lie back completely. Laying down, letting the food digest; staring at the beautiful clouds above. Knowing that you have self-control and a commitment to listening to that inner guidance the inner voice, guiding you too the best foods for you. Guiding you how to eat consciously, guiding you when you feel full and contentment and guiding you when to stop. Deep breathe in hold the breath and exhale let go.

[5 minutes pause]

Now, I am going to guide you back to your consciousness, back to this present moment. Begin to feel your body; begin to feel the space your body is in.

[5 seconds pause]

Wiggle your fingers and toes; relax your jaw; relax your shoulders.

[5 seconds pause]

Twist your body a little; turn your head from side to side.

[5 seconds pause]

Relax. Be aware of any sounds coming from inside or outside the room. And when you are ready, gently open your eyes and come back.

4. Lose Weight effortlessly (60 minutes)

Before we begin, make sure you won't be disturbed for the duration of this meditation. Put your phone and other electronics on "do not disturb" mode. Settle into a position of comfort and ease. Keep your spine straight and alert; your chin parallel to the floor beneath you. Close your eyes. Settle into your body. Take a few deep breaths inhaling from the nose and exhaling from the mouth.
[10 seconds pause]
Continue to breathe in and out deeply on my count this time. Inhale deeply through your nose on the count of 4 – 4, 3, 2, 1. Hold. And exhale through your mouth on the count of 6 – 6, 5, 4, 3, 2, 1.
Again, inhale 4, 3, 2, 1. Hold. And exhale through your mouth on the count of 6 – 6, 5, 4, 3, 2, 1.
Inhale – 4, 3, 2, 1. Hold. And exhale through your mouth on the count of 6 – 6, 5, 4, 3, 2, Relax. Now breathe at your natural rhythmic pace.
[10 seconds pause]
Maintain a gentle awareness on your breath.
[10 seconds pause]
If you find your mind wandering to its own thoughts, gently bring it back to the rhythmic flow of your breath.
[20 seconds pause]
Be aware of your physical body.
[5 seconds pause]
Bring your awareness to your feet. How they feel to you. Are they tired? Do they ache? Flex and wiggle your toes. Allow any tension in your feet to just float away.
[5 seconds pause]
Now focus on your ankles and calves. Feel any stress and tightness that is there, release it and let it go.
[5 seconds pause]
Acknowledge your knees; allow any aching to just gently drift away. Your buttocks and lower back, let the tight feeling of tension begin to unravel and float off.
[5 seconds pause]
Your tummy and abdomen; let go of any twisting and turning that you might be feeling here at this time.
[5 seconds pause]

Feel any tension in your chest. Acknowledge it and set it free. Your shoulders these can hold lot of stress and tightness. Gently and slowly shrug your shoulders, releasing a tension which will relax from shrug.

[5 seconds pause]

Focus on your arms and hands. Clench your fists and then release; let the muscles of your arms relax and tensions flow out from your fingers.

[5 seconds pause]

Now your neck; turn your head slightly to your right now to the left and then right; then back and front; now letting it balance in the centre.

[5 seconds pause]

Now return your awareness to your head and face. Let your jaw fall slightly and your tongue on the gentle resting place behind your teeth.

[5 seconds pause]

Now you have relaxed your body, we are going to go deeper into the relaxation and relax your mind. I am going to count backwards from 10 to 1 and with every number you will deeper into this relaxing meditation. 10, 9,8,7,6,5,4,3,2,1 you are now in a deep state of relaxation.

[5 seconds pause]

Feel the relaxation engulfing your entire being.

[5 seconds pause]

Imagine a beautiful sunny day. You are standing on the edge of a field. It's a beautiful field – full of long grasses and wonderful smelling wild flowers.

[5 seconds pause]

You can notice the bees buzzing and some beautiful butterflies flying all around. You can feel the warmth of the sun on your skin. It does not feel harsh on your skin. The sun's warmth is giving you inner glow and you are feeling refreshed. Your whole body is so light and all the muscles in your body are so relaxed now.

[5 seconds pause]

This beautiful view is giving you a sense of positivity and good feelings. This bright sun is healing all the tiredness and tension in your body.

[5 seconds pause]

You are feeling so light and energetic; so light and energetic. There is a path way cross with a long grass that leads to the old oak trees. You decide to walk along the path. As you move forward, you are witnessing all the beauties of nature. You feel the beautiful flowers with your hands, releasing their fragrance as you touch them. This is giving you a sense of relief. As you move ahead, you feel the coolness and smell of the earth and its texture under your feet. You feel protected. It's a wonderful feeling. You feel relaxed yet so strong.

[5 seconds pause]
Stay in this feeling of relaxation for a while. Know that you are divinely protected.
[30 seconds pause]
Now, it's time to move on to the next part of this meditation where we will focus on our goal to lose weight and reach our ideal shape and size. So, once again, take a few deep breaths inhaling from the nose and exhaling from the mouth.
[10 seconds pause]
Continue to breathe in and out deeply on my count this time. Inhale deeply through your nose on the count of 4 – 4, 3, 2, 1. Hold. And exhale through your mouth on the count of 6 – 6, 5, 4, 3, 2, 1.
Again, inhale 4, 3, 2, 1. Hold. And exhale through your mouth on the count of 6 – 6, 5, 4, 3, 2, 1.
Inhale – 4, 3, 2, 1. Hold. And exhale through your mouth on the count of 6 – 6, 5, 4, 3, 2, Relax. Now breathe at your natural rhythmic pace.
[10 seconds pause]
Maintain a gentle awareness on your breath.
[10 seconds pause]
You are back in your room, back in your body. Now you are completely relaxed and ready to accept the benefits of this meditation.
[10 seconds pause]
I want you to imagine golden-coloured healing energies to descend from above and fill your surroundings. And they wrap you from head to toes, in that beautiful golden colour; protecting and healing, cleansing and clearing every muscle, tissue, fibre, joint, and cell in your body.
[10 seconds pause]
You can feel that the golden healing energy is vibrating very heavily and the more it vibrates the relaxed and healed you feel. These vibrations allow you to easily go into deeper state.
[10 seconds pause]
Relaxed, completely relaxed, you are now in the deepest state of relaxation and peace.
[10 seconds pause]
Welcome the light blue healing light now. And it begins to gently fill the bottoms of your feet with its eternal loving energies. Feel the comfort of healing light entering your body. Has you bring your attention to the bottoms of your feet. Notice what your feet feeling now.
[5 seconds pause]

You may feel warmth, coolness, tingling or nothing much at all. Whatever you feel, it's completely fine. The light blue energy begins to gently move up to your body, through the bottoms of your feet, going into your ankles and calves.

[5 seconds pause]

Now feel the energy moving up into your knees and thighs like a gentle wave of comfort.

[5 seconds pause]

This light blue energy brings healing, strength and energy back into your body. And on its way down feel it cleansing and clearing and washing away all the negatives, all tensions, all blockages.

[5 seconds pause]

Feel it as it fills your lower body with comfort, healing, peace and tranquility. Every muscle, tissue, fiber and bone in your lower body is now vibrating in the light blue healing light.

[5 seconds pause]

Now the light blue healing light gently begins to feel your entire hip area. And while moving up the body feeling the entire abdominal area. Its wraps itself around every internal organ cleansing and clearing, internally and externally All your organs. While the light blue energy cleanses and clears, it energies and heals.

[5 seconds pause]

Relaxation is important to calm your mind down. So whenever you find that your mind has wandered, bring it back to my voice and continue to enjoy this relaxation practice. The light blue energy continues its healing path by moving up your body and wrapping itself around your chest area. Feel your heart, feel it expanding inside your chest now.

[5 seconds pause]

Feel the powerful vibrations from the light blue energy healing your heart from any and all of the past traumas, negative emotions, painful memories, thoughts and feelings. Feel the energy dissolving and removing the old and bringing peace, tranquility and unconditional love back into your heart and body.

[5 seconds pause]

The healing light continues its journey up your body, bringing deeper levels of relaxation into every area. It wraps itself around your lower back. And gently moves up your spine, releasing and relaxing, cleansing and cleaning any points of tension around the spine.

[5 seconds pause]

Feel the muscles on your back now releasing and letting go of all the tensions and stress. Now the light blue energy continues moving up the body from the upper back, to the back of the neck, over the head, dropping down over the facial muscles.

[5 seconds pause]

From your neck the healing power of the light begins to travel down on your arms. From the shoulders down into your elbows, your wrist and through your finger tips and toes like little opening and allowing you to surrender and let go of all the illusions and negative thoughts, feelings and beliefs surround your weight loss. From this point forward each and every day you will find yourself being completely focused on reaching your goal weight.

[5 seconds pause]

As you allow this process to continue, now visualize the eternal loving and healing white light coming down from the universe and connecting with you to the top of your head through your crown chakra and your heart chakra. The minute this connection happens, your entire body becomes filled with universal love and energy.

[5 seconds pause]

Your entire body begins to vibrate in this white light on the deepest secular love. And through this vibration your entire mind and body continues to cleanse and clear, heal, restore and rejuvenate, shedding away all the extra and unwanted fat.

[5 seconds pause]

Feel the healing energy is reverberating inside of you. It is stimulating your goal of weight loss, gently beginning to dissolve the extra pounds from your body. When you welcome the healing energies into your life, you will notice that the positive that your weight loose journey has become smoother and more effortless.

[5 seconds pause]

Stay in this feeling for a while

[10 minutes]

Visualize yourself standing at the top of a staircase. This staircase has 5 steps which you are about to descend now, one by one. And with each step you take, two things will happen – one, you will get more relaxed, and two, you will lose the extra weight from your body. So, with each step deepen your feeling of relaxation and also visualize yourself becoming slimmer and fitter.

[5 seconds pause]

Five: Feeling calm, feeling peaceful, and feeling light. You get slimmer as you see your body shedding the unwanted fat.

Four: You take one more step and enter into a deeper state of relaxation. You continue to lose your extra fat.

Three: More relaxed and more calm. You can see yourself getting nearer to your perfect body.

Two: Even more relaxed and peaceful. The improvement in your body and physique are quite visible now.

One: Into the deepest state of relaxation and calmness. You are now at your exact ideal size.

Zero: You descend the stairs and see that in front of you is a mirror. You look into the mirror and see yourself at your ideal weight, shape, and size.

[5 seconds pause]

Feel how vibrant and healthy you look at your ideal weight. See as vividly as you can. See yourself dressed beautifully standing tall and confident, looking spectacular.

[5 seconds pause]

From now on, you will keep this image of your ideal self in your mind. It should be the first picture that comes to your mind the moment you wake up, it should stay with you throughout the day, and you should visualize this picture before you go to sleep. And you will notice that with time, you will begin to associate more with your ideal self and you will effortlessly move on the path leading to weight loss. You will automatically choose healthy and fresh fruits, vegetables and food items over unhealthy and fatty food. You will feel the motivation to exercise and keep yourself physically fit. The more you visualize this image, the more you will find ways to become that ideal self – smoothly and effortlessly.

[5 seconds pause]

I want you spend some time with this ideal image. Give your imagination a free run. Visualize the whole process and the end result exactly how you want it to happen. Remember, the more deeply you feel it, the more effortlessly you will achieve it. If you can conceive it in your mind, it will definitely turn into reality one day.

[5 seconds pause]

Get into your zone of imagination. Tap into your power of creativity. Bask into the feelings of your ideal self.

[20 minutes pause]

Now, I will be counting from one to ten. And when I reach ten, I want you to open your eyes and be fully aware.

One: You are conscious of your existence. You are listening to my voice with full awareness. Even if you were un-attentive during the hypnosis, you have now complete awareness of each word that I say. Your subconscious mind was active and has received my messages. It is working out to find ways to bring you the desired results. So, now you can come back. Follow my voice.

Two: You can now listen to your mind's chatter. You can hear hour thoughts. The internal dialogue is audible to you. Be relaxed. Be aware. Be relaxed. Be aware. Be relaxed. Be aware.

Three: You are aware of the space you are in. You can feel your physical body. You are back in the reality now; back in the real world.

Four: You can feel the outer layer of your body. You can the texture of the clothing touching your skin.

Five: You can now notice your sense of smell. Can you smell anything peculiar? Or is it plain air that you breathe?

Six: And can you hear the noises coming from outside the room? Any noise from inside the room?

Seven: Feel your body. Feel your feet, your legs, and your hips. Feel your abdomen and your chest region. Feel your entire spinal column, feel your back. Be aware of your hands and wrists and your elbows and your entire arms. Now your shoulders and neck and chin. Now bring your awareness into your entire face. Feel your eyes resting in your sockets; now your forehead and your scalp. In a moment, be aware of your entire physical body.

Eight: And you are back, back in your senses, back in the present moment. You know that anytime you open your eyes, you will be back. So you are ready now. Feel the confidence in your body. Feel the flow of energy in your body.

Nine: You are aware of the present moment, be here of the now. This present moment is the reality. You are back. Be aware of your breathing. Be aware of the in-breath. Be aware of the out-breath. Be aware of the in-breath. Be aware of the out-breath. Very good! Be aware of the in-breath. Be aware of the out-breath.

Ten: Coming back completely into the physical awareness, feel your presence, feel your being. Bring your hands to your eyes and gently massage them. Now you return to your consciousness. Blink your eyes. Gently, very gently open your eyes. Welcome Back!

III. Quit Smoking Affirmations

5. Affirmations for Healthy Eating Habits (40 minutes)

We have this amazing ability to turn thoughts into reality. That's why sages as well as scientists all recommend focusing on what we think and what we say. We must always choose our words wisely because they have the latent power to turn our fortunes. In today's meditation, we are going to work on inculcating healthy eating habits for weight loss and good health through the power of affirmations. Let's first relax the body so that the subconscious mind is in a better state to receive and act on the messages.
[5 seconds pause]
Take three deep and long breaths. Fill your lungs with air. Let go and relax as you breathe out.
[5 seconds pause]
Breathe even deeper. And then release it slowly at the out breath.
[5 seconds pause]
Just notice how your body is feeling now, without trying to change it.
[5 seconds pause]
Notice your emotions, without trying to shift them.
[5 seconds pause]
Notice the areas of tension and heaviness in the body. Notice the areas of space and freedom in the body. Feel your whole body without any manipulation. Accept how it feels, accept whatever sensations are arising.
[5 seconds pause]
Feel relaxed. Feel free. Take your attention to the top of your head. Welcome the awareness of the sensations at the top of your head. Notice the different feelings, tension, itchiness, numbness. Notice other sensations on your scalp. Gently scan the scalp and notice what arises.
[5 seconds pause]
Pay attention on purpose. Notice the forehead; feel the eyes; feel the mouth and the lips.
[5 seconds pause]
Now feel the sensations of your cheeks; feel the sensations of the whole face.
[5 seconds pause]
Being with these sensations is being in connection with your own self.

[5 seconds pause]
Take your attention to any sensations of your throat. Bring your attention to your shoulder and your chest. Notice all the tiny, subtle feelings in the parts of your body that you don't usually pay attention to. Now is the time to do so.
[5 seconds pause]
Noticing and connecting with the feelings in your arms. Notice the feeling in your fingers and your hands. Feel your abdomen, noticing the sensation in your belly. Feel, observe and accept whatever arises.
[5 seconds pause]
Bring your awareness to the back of the shoulders, travelling down the back, through all the different layers of sensations.
[5 seconds pause]
Feel the middle back. Feel the lower back. Feel the seat of the body. Connecting with the feelings with your hips and bringing that attention down to the thighs. Exploring, noticing, and being curious. Take your attention to your knees, feeling the front of the knee as well as the back of the knee and now your shins.
[5 seconds pause]
Notice the sensations in the calves. Connect with the sensations with the top of your feet.
[5 seconds pause]
And now feel the soles of your feet.
[5 seconds pause]
Now let's connect with the whole body; observing and feeling the full landscape; feeling connected, feeling whole, feeling safe.
[5 seconds pause]
You are protected; you are safe; you are being looked after.
[5 minutes pause]
Now, I want you to repeat these affirmations with me with full intent and focus.
I welcome new healthy habits. I am becoming stronger mentally and physically. I am flexible. I am full of life. Change is easy for me. I eat natural foods. I am safe and trusty. I am aware of and listen to my intuitions. I am ready for success. I am the creator of my own life. I am grateful for my health and my amazing body. It is such a miracle I see the beauty of my body just as it is. I am kind to myself.
[5 seconds pause]
I welcome new healthy habits. I am becoming stronger mentally and physically. I am flexible. I am full of life. Change is easy for me. I eat natural foods. I am safe and trusty. I am aware of and listen to my intuitions. I am ready for success. I am the creator of my own

life. I am grateful for my health and my amazing body. It is such a miracle I see the beauty of my body just as it is. I am kind to myself.

[5 seconds pause]

I welcome new healthy habits. I am becoming stronger mentally and physically. I am flexible. I am full of life. Change is easy for me. I eat natural foods. I am safe and trusty. I am aware of and listen to my intuitions. I am ready for success. I am the creator of my own life. I am grateful for my health and my amazing body. It is such a miracle I see the beauty of my body just as it is. I am kind to myself.

[15 seconds pause]

I am open to new ways of eating healthy. I am patient with myself and others. I appreciate of any gift of help and support. I lighten up mentally and physically. I choose food that truly nourishes me. I eat slowly and mindfully. My energy is becoming lighter and brighter every day. I enjoy taking good care of myself. I invest in myself and in my health. I trust myself and the process of life. I can do anything I set my mind to. I respond all trigger with awareness and kindness.

[5 seconds pause]

I am open to new ways of eating healthy. I am patient with myself and others. I appreciate of any gift of help and support. I lighten up mentally and physically. I choose food that truly nourishes me. I eat slowly and mindfully. My energy is becoming lighter and brighter every day. I enjoy taking good care of myself. I invest in myself and in my health. I trust myself and the process of life. I can do anything I set my mind to. I respond all trigger with awareness and kindness.

[5 seconds pause]

I am open to new ways of eating healthy. I am patient with myself and others. I appreciate of any gift of help and support. I lighten up mentally and physically. I choose food that truly nourishes me. I eat slowly and mindfully. My energy is becoming lighter and brighter every day. I enjoy taking good care of myself. I invest in myself and in my health. I trust myself and the process of life. I can do anything I set my mind to. I respond all trigger with awareness and kindness.

[15 seconds pause]

I enjoy working out. I am successful and managing my weight and managing my stress. I say yes to life. Change is good for me. My actions and behavior support my perfect weight. I am flexible mentally and physically. I listen to my body. I listen to my intuition. I see my body as an amazing miracle. I enjoy the variety of wholesome foods. I can control my body and give it only healthy food. I have a strong immune system. Any change is easy for me.

[5 seconds pause]

I enjoy working out. I am successful and managing my weight and managing my stress. I say yes to life. Change is good for me. My actions and behavior support my perfect weight. I am flexible mentally and physically. I listen to my body. I listen to my intuition. I see my body as an amazing miracle. I enjoy the variety of wholesome foods. I can control my body and give it only healthy food. I have a strong immune system. Any change is easy for me.

[5 seconds pause]

I enjoy working out. I am successful and managing my weight and managing my stress. I say yes to life. Change is good for me. My actions and behavior support my perfect weight. I am flexible mentally and physically. I listen to my body. I listen to my intuition. I see my body as an amazing miracle. I enjoy the variety of wholesome foods. I can control my body and give it only healthy food. I have a strong immune system. Any change is easy for me.

[15 seconds pause]

I make healthy choices to support all the work my body does. I am relaxed and at peace. I love the taste of healthy food. I am satisfied with just a right amount of food. I am ready to shed the burdens of the past. My body and mind are relaxed and in perfect harmony. I move forward with love and gratitude. All my thoughts help me to be healthier. I am grateful for my health. It is easy for me to ask for support.

[5 seconds pause]

I make healthy choices to support all the work my body does. I am relaxed and at peace. I love the taste of healthy food. I am satisfied with just a right amount of food. I am ready to shed the burdens of the past. My body and mind are relaxed and in perfect harmony. I move forward with love and gratitude. All my thoughts help me to be healthier. I am grateful for my health. It is easy for me to ask for support.

[5 seconds pause]

I make healthy choices to support all the work my body does. I am relaxed and at peace. I love the taste of healthy food. I am satisfied with just a right amount of food. I am ready to shed the burdens of the past. My body and mind are relaxed and in perfect harmony. I move forward with love and gratitude. All my thoughts help me to be healthier. I am grateful for my health. It is easy for me to ask for support.

[15 seconds pause]

I start and end each day with gratitude. I like to keep track of my eating and exercise. It is easy to make smart choices. I feel my feelings. I listen to my body, when its needs rest, hydration and nutrition. I am a confident, happy and optimistic person and laugh often. I feel safe in my healthy and changing body. I have a healthy attitude towards all types of foods.

[5 seconds pause]

I start and end each day with gratitude. I like to keep track of my eating and exercise. It is easy to make smart choices. I feel my feelings. I listen to my body, when its needs rest, hydration and nutrition. I am a confident, happy and optimistic person and laugh often.I feel safe in my healthy and changing body. I have a healthy attitude towards all types of foods.

[5 seconds pause]

I start and end each day with gratitude. I like to keep track of my eating and exercise. It is easy to make smart choices. I feel my feelings. I listen to my body, when its needs rest, hydration and nutrition. I am a confident, happy and optimistic person and laugh often.I feel safe in my healthy and changing body. I have a healthy attitude towards all types of foods.

[15 seconds pause]

I respect my body and my health. I love food with vital life force energy. I create a new healthier meal. I am safe, secure and grounded. Positive thinking leads to positive results. I have help for the future. I feel safe in a healthier lighter body. I only need to feed my body better amount of food. I attract positive people and events into my life. I am grateful for my amazing body and my health.

[5 seconds pause]

I respect my body and my health. I love food with vital life force energy. I create a new healthier meal. I am safe, secure and grounded. Positive thinking leads to positive results. I have help for the future. I feel safe in a healthier lighter body. I only need to feed my body better amount of food. I attract positive people and events into my life. I am grateful for my amazing body and my health.

[5 seconds pause]

I respect my body and my health. I love food with vital life force energy. I create a new healthier meal. I am safe, secure and grounded. Positive thinking leads to positive results. I have help for the future. I feel safe in a healthier lighter body. I only need to feed my body better amount of food. I attract positive people and events into my life. I am grateful for my amazing body and my health.

[15 seconds pause]

I choose to focus on what is good in my life. I am letting go of the emotional weight from the past. My life is lighter and brighter. I forget my past and let it go. Meditation is good for me. I can master my weight and my stress now and forever. I am creating more balance in my life. I am in the perfect place here now. I love myself unconditionally. I enjoy deep healing sleep. I am able to restore and reset with sleep.

[5 seconds pause]

I choose to focus on what is good in my life. I am letting go of the emotional weight from the past. My life is lighter and brighter. I forget my past and let it go. Meditation is good for me. I can master my weight and my stress now and forever. I am creating more balance in my life. I am in the perfect place here now. I love myself unconditionally. I enjoy deep healing sleep. I am able to restore and reset with sleep.

[5 seconds pause]

I choose to focus on what is good in my life. I am letting go of the emotional weight from the past. My life is lighter and brighter. I forget my past and let it go. Meditation is good for me. I can master my weight and my stress now and forever. I am creating more balance in my life. I am in the perfect place here now. I love myself unconditionally. I enjoy deep healing sleep. I am able to restore and reset with sleep.

[15 seconds pause]

I prioritize my health and wellbeing. I invest in myself and my health. I sleep soundly. I choose to be happy right now. I love bring balance into my life. I tune in to the rhythm of nature. I am in a process of creating a healthier meal. I approve of myself. Every day and every way I am becoming a healthier, happier me. I only think positively and visualize it positively. I enjoy learning new ways of becoming happier.

[5 seconds pause]

I prioritize my health and wellbeing. I invest in myself and my health. I sleep soundly. I choose to be happy right now. I love bring balance into my life. I tune in to the rhythm of nature. I am in a process of creating a healthier meal. I approve of myself. Every day and every way I am becoming a healthier, happier me. I only think positively and visualize it positively. I enjoy learning new ways of becoming happier.

[5 seconds pause]

I prioritize my health and wellbeing. I invest in myself and my health. I sleep soundly. I choose to be happy right now. I love bring balance into my life. I tune in to the rhythm of nature. I am in a process of creating a healthier meal. I approve of myself. Every day and every way I am becoming a healthier, happier me. I only think positively and visualize it positively. I enjoy learning new ways of becoming happier.

[15 seconds pause]

I can do anything I set my mind to. I am healthy and whole. I nourish my body with healthy and fresh food. I am energized. Exercise is fun for me. I lighten up mentally and physically. I am open to change. I enjoy taking good care of myself. I love to be flexible spontaneous. I know that I can shape my body according to how I want. I am a happy person to be around. I am relaxed and calm.

[5 seconds pause]

I can do anything I set my mind to. I am healthy and whole. I nourish my body with healthy and fresh food. I am energized. Exercise is fun for me. I lighten up mentally and physically. I am open to change. I enjoy taking good care of myself. I love to be flexible spontaneous. I know that I can shape my body according to how I want. I am a happy person to be around. I am relaxed and calm.

[5 seconds pause]

I can do anything I set my mind to. I am healthy and whole. I nourish my body with healthy and fresh food. I am energized. Exercise is fun for me. I lighten up mentally and physically. I am open to change. I enjoy taking good care of myself. I love to be flexible spontaneous. I know that I can shape my body according to how I want. I am a happy person to be around. I am relaxed and calm.

[15 seconds pause]

I am exploring and moving on to new ways of eating healthy that I enjoy. I am obtaining wonderful things that were not possible before it. I am creative. I am connected with all force for higher good. I am light hearted. I am forgiving and flexible. I am hopeful and optimistic. I am contend and serene. I am ready for success. I am grateful for my health and my amazing body. I am kind to myself. I speak to myself with kindness and compassion. I am patient with myself. I choose food that truly nourishes me. I eat mindfully, slowly.

[5 seconds pause]

I am exploring and moving on to new ways of eating healthy that I enjoy. I am obtaining wonderful things that were not possible before it. I am creative. I am connected with all force for higher good. I am light hearted. I am forgiving and flexible. I am hopeful and optimistic. I am contend and serene. I am ready for success. I am grateful for my health and my amazing body. I am kind to myself. I speak to myself with kindness and compassion. I am patient with myself. I choose food that truly nourishes me. I eat mindfully, slowly.

[5 seconds pause]

I am exploring and moving on to new ways of eating healthy that I enjoy. I am obtaining wonderful things that were not possible before it. I am creative. I am connected with all force for higher good. I am light hearted. I am forgiving and flexible. I am hopeful and optimistic. I am contend and serene. I am ready for success. I am grateful for my health and my amazing body. I am kind to myself. I speak to myself with kindness and compassion. I am patient with myself. I choose food that truly nourishes me. I eat mindfully, slowly.

[15 seconds pause]

My whole body works in perfect harmony. I am in a process to bringing balance to my body. I am light hearted. I trust myself to choose the right choices in food. i choose positive thoughts. I am a complete and whole person. I arrange my life to make it easier for me to eat healthy activities. I am hopeful. Peace, love and all acceptances flow through me. I forgive and let go what is not good for me.

[5 seconds pause]

My whole body works in perfect harmony. I am in a process to bringing balance to my body. I am light hearted. I trust myself to choose the right choices in food. i choose positive thoughts. I am a complete and whole person. I arrange my life to make it easier for me to eat healthy activities. I am hopeful. Peace, love and all acceptances flow through me. I forgive and let go what is not good for me.

[5 seconds pause]

My whole body works in perfect harmony. I am in a process to bringing balance to my body. I am light hearted. I trust myself to choose the right choices in food. i choose positive thoughts. I am a complete and whole person. I arrange my life to make it easier for me to eat healthy activities. I am hopeful. Peace, love and all acceptances flow through me. I forgive and let go what is not good for me.

[15 seconds pause]

I invest in myself and in my health. I have control over my emotions. It's safe for me to say my feelings. There are many healthy ways to comfort myself. I respond appropriately to all my emotions. I feel good about myself. I enjoy my own company. I release that need to criticize and compare myself. I am open to new experiences. I am enthusiastic to my new healthy habits. It's easy for me to reach and maintain my perfect weight for me. I feel free because I am free. I see the beauty of my body.

[5 seconds pause]

I invest in myself and in my health. I have control over my emotions. It's safe for me to say my feelings. There are many healthy ways to comfort myself. I respond appropriately to all my emotions. I feel good about myself. I enjoy my own company. I release that need to criticize and compare myself. I am open to new experiences. I am enthusiastic to my new healthy habits. It's easy for me to reach and maintain my perfect weight for me. I feel free because I am free. I see the beauty of my body.

[5 seconds pause]

I invest in myself and in my health. I have control over my emotions. It's safe for me to say my feelings. There are many healthy ways to comfort myself. I respond appropriately to all my emotions. I feel good about myself. I enjoy my own company. I release that need to criticize and compare myself. I am open to new experiences. I am enthusiastic to my new healthy habits. It's easy for me to reach and maintain my perfect weight for me. I feel free because I am free. I see the beauty of my body.

[15 seconds pause]

I am filled with vitality. I am satisfied with right amount of food. When I feel full it's easy to put down my fork. My body and mind are relaxed. I peacefully release excess weight. I radiate health and positivity. I am willing to change. I love the lightness of my mind and body. With every day that passes, I look better and more alive. I am in a process of rejuvenation. I see all the beauty that surrounds me even when I look in the mirror. I am responsible for my health and mind.

[5 seconds pause]

I am filled with vitality. I am satisfied with right amount of food. When I feel full it's easy to put down my fork. My body and mind are relaxed. I peacefully release excess weight. I radiate health and positivity. I am willing to change. I love the lightness of my mind and body. With every day that passes, I look better and more alive. I am in a process of rejuvenation. I see all the beauty that surrounds me even when I look in the mirror. I am responsible for my health and mind.

[5 seconds pause]

I am filled with vitality. I am satisfied with right amount of food. When I feel full it's easy to put down my fork. My body and mind are relaxed. I peacefully release excess weight. I radiate health and positivity. I am willing to change. I love the lightness of my mind and body. With every day that passes, I look better and more alive. I am in a process of rejuvenation. I see all the beauty that surrounds me even when I look in the mirror. I am responsible for my health and mind.

[15 seconds pause]

Wellness is the natural state of my body. I embrace change. I love the way I reach my goals. I love eating natural foods. I am grateful for every new day, a fresh start and a chance to begin again. My body is more relaxed. All is well in my world. I eat nutrient-rich and healthy food. I have exercise a part of my daily routine. My efforts to lose weight are showing good results. I am happy with my progress. I have achieved the perfect size and weight. My body, mind and emotions are in balance and harmony. I am in happy, healthy, and completely fit.

[5 seconds pause]

Wellness is the natural state of my body. I embrace change. I love the way I reach my goals. I love eating natural foods. I am grateful for every new day, a fresh start and a chance to begin again. My body is more relaxed. All is well in my world. I eat nutrient-rich and healthy food. I have exercise a part of my daily routine. My efforts to lose weight are showing good results. I am happy with my progress. I have achieved the perfect size and weight. My body, mind and emotions are in balance and harmony. I am in happy, healthy, and completely fit.

[5 seconds pause]

Wellness is the natural state of my body. I embrace change. I love the way I reach my goals. I love eating natural foods. I am grateful for every new day, a fresh start and a chance to begin again. My body is more relaxed. All is well in my world. I eat nutrient-rich and healthy food. I have exercise a part of my daily routine. My efforts to lose weight are showing good results. I am happy with my progress. I have achieved the perfect size and weight. My body, mind and emotions are in balance and harmony. I am in happy, healthy, and completely fit.

6. Affirmations for Rapid Weight loss (60 minutes)

Hello and a warm welcome to this session of meditation. Today, we will focus on achieving our goal of losing weight through affirmations. The power of positive intentions and affirmations should never be underestimated because what we think about repeatedly manifests into reality. Before we begin, I want you to be completely relaxed and at ease. A calm mind will ensure that you focus on nothing else but the words for your goal achievement. Starting with a relaxing breathing and body scan exercise, we will move on the affirmation part. We will say a few lines together and then repeat the same lines two more times to multiply the powerful impact of those words and intentions. So, for now, simply relax and let go of any thoughts that no longer serve you. Forget about what has happened. Do not worry about what's about to come. Just focus on the present moment.

[5 seconds pause]

Give yourself permission to arrive. Pay attention. So allow your breath to move in through your nose and out through your nose and let this contribute to your concentration.

[5 seconds pause]

Be aware of what is happening now so you know your breath in and your breath out and with each breath you get clear, you are here. As you allow yourself to feel the breathing body and, give yourself a moment to feel relieved.

[5 seconds pause]

Notice whatever comes up in your and keep returning to your breath. And as you tap in the well spring of breathing way you feel the blessing and gift of each breath.

[5 seconds pause]

Feel the ebb and flow of your breath. Be present. So whatever is happening before and whatever will be revealed later you tap into this moment with gratitude you are still here. Breathing in and breathing out.

[5 seconds pause]

Relax your body; loosen up your muscles, relax your shoulders, relax your jaw.

Release any stress that may be stored in your body. Relax; completely relax.

[5 minutes pause]

Now repeat these affirmations after me.

"My body is rapidly responding to my actions efforts for weight loss. My body repairs itself constantly. I eat to nourish my body. I am learning more about my body every day. I keep track of my success. I love walking and being active. I am free to let go of excess weight. I enjoy the lightness of my being. I eat to nourish my body. I love my body unconditionally. I release the past and let it go and ready to fresh start."

[5 seconds pause]

"My body is rapidly responding to my actions efforts for weight loss. My body repairs itself constantly. I eat to nourish my body. I am learning more about my body every day. I keep track of my success. I love walking and being active. I am free to let go of excess weight. I enjoy the lightness of my being. I eat to nourish my body. I love my body unconditionally. I release the past and let it go and ready to fresh start."

[5 seconds pause]

"My body is rapidly responding to my actions efforts for weight loss. My body repairs itself constantly. I eat to nourish my body. I am learning more about my body every day. I keep track of my success. I love walking and being active. I am free to let go of excess weight. I enjoy the lightness of my being. I eat to nourish my body. I love my body unconditionally. I release the past and let it go and ready to fresh start."

[15 seconds pause]

I am losing unnecessary fat muscles with each day. I make healthy choices. My cells are healthy and happy. I nourish my body with healthy whole fresh food. I am filled with enthusiasm and energy. I love to exercise in a way that that is fun for me. I am lightening up mentally and physically. I am open to change and flexibility. I am relaxed and calmed. I set behavioral goals to achieve the way that is just right for me.

[5 seconds pause]

I am losing unnecessary fat muscles with each day. I make healthy choices. My cells are healthy and happy. I nourish my body with healthy whole fresh food. I am filled with enthusiasm and energy. I love to exercise in a way that that is fun for me. I am lightening up mentally and physically. I am open to change and flexibility. I am relaxed and calmed. I set behavioral goals to achieve the way that is just right for me.

[5 seconds pause]

I am losing unnecessary fat muscles with each day. I make healthy choices. My cells are healthy and happy. I nourish my body with healthy whole fresh food. I am filled with enthusiasm and energy. I love to exercise in a way that that is fun for me. I am lightening up mentally and physically. I am open to change and flexibility. I am relaxed and calmed. I set behavioral goals to achieve the way that is just right for me.

[15 seconds pause]

My whole energy system is changing for a slimmer, fitter me. My natural energy is increasing. I am strong and healthy. I chose to drink more water and I stay hydrated. I have a strong immune system. I set specific and achievable goals. I love to have exercise makes my body and mind fill. I eat only what I need. I enjoy fun ways to exercise. I love eating more fruits and vegetables. I find healthy ways to comforts myself.

[5 seconds pause]

My whole energy system is changing for a slimmer, fitter me. My natural energy is increasing. I am strong and healthy. I chose to drink more water and I stay hydrated. I have a strong immune system. I set specific and achievable goals. I love to have exercise makes my body and mind fill. I eat only what I need. I enjoy fun ways to exercise. I love eating more fruits and vegetables. I find healthy ways to comforts myself.

[5 seconds pause]

My whole energy system is changing for a slimmer, fitter me. My natural energy is increasing. I am strong and healthy. I chose to drink more water and I stay hydrated. I have a strong immune system. I set specific and achievable goals. I love to have exercise makes my body and mind fill. I eat only what I need. I enjoy fun ways to exercise. I love eating more fruits and vegetables. I find healthy ways to comforts myself.

[15 seconds pause]

I am in control of my diet. My emotions come and go with ease. Emotions are just energy. I am aware of my thoughts and emotions. I can respond appropriately to all of my emotions. I eat slowly and mindfully. There are many healthy ways to comfort myself. I am open to possibilities and new experiences. I am getting more attractive and energetic I believe in myself and in my possibilities.

[5 seconds pause]

I am in control of my diet. My emotions come and go with ease. Emotions are just energy. I am aware of my thoughts and emotions. I can respond appropriately to all of my emotions. I eat slowly and mindfully. There are many healthy ways to comfort myself. I am open to possibilities and new experiences. I am getting more attractive and energetic I believe in myself and in my possibilities.

[5 seconds pause]

I am in control of my diet. My emotions come and go with ease. Emotions are just energy. I am aware of my thoughts and emotions. I can respond appropriately to all of my emotions. I eat slowly and mindfully. There are many healthy ways to comfort myself. I am open to possibilities and new experiences. I am getting more attractive and energetic I believe in myself and in my possibilities.

[15 seconds pause]

I eat only when I am hungry. My body is responding to I see all the beauty of my amazing body when I look in the mirror or look at the photograph. I love and care for my body. Meditation helps me reaches and maintain my perfect weight. I see that beauty of my body.

My body is such a miracle. I make healthy choices to support my miraculous body. I allow myself to be happy and healthy. I don't need to eat too much, cakes and things with sugar.

[5 seconds pause]

I eat only when I am hungry. My body is responding to I see all the beauty of my amazing body when I look in the mirror or look at the photograph. I love and care for my body. Meditation helps me reaches and maintain my perfect weight. I see that beauty of my body. My body is such a miracle. I make healthy choices to support my miraculous body. I allow myself to be happy and healthy. I don't need to eat too much, cakes and things with sugar.

[5 seconds pause]

I eat only when I am hungry. My body is responding to I see all the beauty of my amazing body when I look in the mirror or look at the photograph. I love and care for my body. Meditation helps me reaches and maintain my perfect weight. I see that beauty of my body. My body is such a miracle. I make healthy choices to support my miraculous body. I allow myself to be happy and healthy. I don't need to eat too much, cakes and things with sugar.

[15 seconds pause]

I accept new healthy habits into my life. I radiate positivity and vitality. I learn new healthy ways easily. I appreciate my progress. I am grateful for my amazing body. I learn from all my behaviors and choices. I welcome new healthy habits. I acknowledge all my achievements. I feel good about myself. I move forward to new healthy habits. I love to take time to relax.

[5 seconds pause]

I accept new healthy habits into my life. I radiate positivity and vitality. I learn new healthy ways easily. I appreciate my progress. I am grateful for my amazing body. I learn from all my behaviors and choices. I welcome new healthy habits. I acknowledge all my achievements. I feel good about myself. I move forward to new healthy habits. I love to take time to relax.

[5 seconds pause]

I accept new healthy habits into my life. I radiate positivity and vitality. I learn new healthy ways easily. I appreciate my progress. I am grateful for my amazing body. I learn from all my behaviors and choices. I welcome new healthy habits. I acknowledge all my achievements. I feel good about myself. I move forward to new healthy habits. I love to take time to relax.

[15 seconds pause]

I love reaching my exercise goals. I eat only when I feel physically hungry. I peacefully release excess weight. I radiate health and vitality. I feel free and light. I am free to let go of the past. I choose to drink more water. I enjoy fruits and vegetables. I am willing to change. I am lightening up mentally and physically. I love the lightness of my body and mind. I am in the process of rejuvenating of every level.

[5 seconds pause]

I love reaching my exercise goals. I eat only when I feel physically hungry. I peacefully release excess weight. I radiate health and vitality. I feel free and light. I am free to let go of the past. I choose to drink more water. I enjoy fruits and vegetables. I am willing to change. I am lightening up mentally and physically. I love the lightness of my body and mind. I am in the process of rejuvenating of every level.

[5 seconds pause]

I love reaching my exercise goals. I eat only when I feel physically hungry. I peacefully release excess weight. I radiate health and vitality. I feel free and light. I am free to let go of the past. I choose to drink more water. I enjoy fruits and vegetables. I am willing to change. I am lightening up mentally and physically. I love the lightness of my body and mind. I am in the process of rejuvenating of every level.

[15 seconds pause]

I am excited about a new way of being slimmer and lighter. I love foods that are alive with nutrients. I am responsible for my own health and happiness. I enjoy trying new healthy activities. My whole body works in perfect harmony. I speak to myself with kindness and compassion. I am patient with myself. I am full of compassion for myself.

[5 seconds pause]

I am excited about a new way of being slimmer and lighter. I love foods that are alive with nutrients. I am responsible for my own health and happiness. I enjoy trying new healthy activities. My whole body works in perfect harmony. I speak to myself with kindness and compassion. I am patient with myself. I am full of compassion for myself.

[5 seconds pause]

I am excited about a new way of being slimmer and lighter. I love foods that are alive with nutrients. I am responsible for my own health and happiness. I enjoy trying new healthy activities. My whole body works in perfect harmony. I speak to myself with kindness and compassion. I am patient with myself. I am full of compassion for myself.

[15 seconds pause]

I trust myself to make the right food choices for me. Change is good for me. I absorb nutrients easily. I create a nurturing environment that allows me to enjoy a healthy life style. I am confident and capable. I am in a process in bringing balance to my life. I am open minded and flexible. I eat mindfully and enjoy every nutritious bite. I reward myself in fun and healthy ways. I am blessed with an abundant life.

[5 seconds pause]

I trust myself to make the right food choices for me. Change is good for me. I absorb nutrients easily. I create a nurturing environment that allows me to enjoy a healthy life style. I am confident and capable. I am in a process in bringing balance to my life. I am open minded and flexible. I eat mindfully and enjoy every nutritious bite. I reward myself in fun and healthy ways. I am blessed with an abundant life.

[5 seconds pause]

I trust myself to make the right food choices for me. Change is good for me. I absorb nutrients easily. I create a nurturing environment that allows me to enjoy a healthy life style. I am confident and capable. I am in a process in bringing balance to my life. I am open minded and flexible. I eat mindfully and enjoy every nutritious bite. I reward myself in fun and healthy ways. I am blessed with an abundant life.

[15 seconds pause]

I enjoy eating natural foods. My mind and body are in perfect harmony. It is healthy for me to feel my feelings with patience and loving awareness. I am full of gratitude for my healthy life. I choose positive thoughts. I easily ask for help and support. I love taking good care of myself. I see opportunities for healthy life everywhere. I am complete and whole person. I face both good and bad feelings with ease.

[5 seconds pause]

I enjoy eating natural foods. My mind and body are in perfect harmony. It is healthy for me to feel my feelings with patience and loving awareness. I am full of gratitude for my healthy life. I choose positive thoughts. I easily ask for help and support. I love taking good care of myself. I see opportunities for healthy life everywhere. I am complete and whole person. I face both good and bad feelings with ease.

[5 seconds pause]

I enjoy eating natural foods. My mind and body are in perfect harmony. It is healthy for me to feel my feelings with patience and loving awareness. I am full of gratitude for my healthy life. I choose positive thoughts. I easily ask for help and support. I love taking good care of myself. I see opportunities for healthy life everywhere. I am complete and whole person. I face both good and bad feelings with ease.

[15 seconds pause]

I arrange my life to make it easy to have healthy activities. I am confident and courageous. I move forward with my new healthy habits. I am calm and at peace with myself. I embrace change. When I achieve a goal I pat myself on the back and set a new goal. I am glowing with health and energy.

[5 seconds pause]

I arrange my life to make it easy to have healthy activities. I am confident and courageous. I move forward with my new healthy habits. I am calm and at peace with myself. I embrace change. When I achieve a goal I pat myself on the back and set a new goal. I am glowing with health and energy.

[5 seconds pause]

I arrange my life to make it easy to have healthy activities. I am confident and courageous. I move forward with my new healthy habits. I am calm and at peace with myself. I embrace change. When I achieve a goal I pat myself on the back and set a new goal. I am glowing with health and energy.

[15 seconds pause]

I am losing extra weight effortlessly and rapidly. I am honest and loving and peaceful. I live a wholesome balanced life. I am open to possibilities. I am creative and enthusiastic. I am a positive person. I powerfully manifest a healthy body and mind. I am peaceful and calm. Change is good for me. I am spontaneous and flexible.

[5 seconds pause]

I am losing extra weight effortlessly and rapidly. I am honest and loving and peaceful. I live a wholesome balanced life. I am open to possibilities. I am creative and enthusiastic. I am a positive person. I powerfully manifest a healthy body and mind. I am peaceful and calm. Change is good for me. I am spontaneous and flexible.

[5 seconds pause]

I am losing extra weight effortlessly and rapidly. I am honest and loving and peaceful. I live a wholesome balanced life. I am open to possibilities. I am creative and enthusiastic. I am a positive person. I powerfully manifest a healthy body and mind. I am peaceful and calm. Change is good for me. I am spontaneous and flexible.

[15 seconds pause]

I release extra weight easily. My self-awareness is expanding. I am filled with passion and purpose. Food is fuel and enhances the healing process. I see all the beauty that surrounds me. I am expanding self-awareness. I rest my body when it is tired. I feed my body when it needs nourishment. Meditation creates calmness and clears my thinking.

[5 seconds pause]

I release extra weight easily. My self-awareness is expanding. I am filled with passion and purpose. Food is fuel and enhances the healing process. I see all the beauty that surrounds me. I am expanding self-awareness. I rest my body when it is tired. I feed my body when it needs nourishment. Meditation creates calmness and clears my thinking.

[5 seconds pause]

I release extra weight easily. My self-awareness is expanding. I am filled with passion and purpose. Food is fuel and enhances the healing process. I see all the beauty that surrounds me. I am expanding self-awareness. I rest my body when it is tired. I feed my body when it needs nourishment. Meditation creates calmness and clears my thinking.

[15 seconds pause]

My happiness comes from being healthy. When I reach for food I am able to pause and respond properly. I eat only when I am hungry. I love and accept myself unconditionally. I am ready to release extra weight that no longer serves me. I release mental weight. I release emotional weight.

[5 seconds pause]

My happiness comes from being healthy. When I reach for food I am able to pause and respond properly. I eat only when I am hungry. I love and accept myself unconditionally. I am ready to release extra weight that no longer serves me. I release mental weight. I release emotional weight.

[5 seconds pause]

My happiness comes from being healthy. When I reach for food I am able to pause and respond properly. I eat only when I am hungry. I love and accept myself unconditionally. I am ready to release extra weight that no longer serves me. I release mental weight. I release emotional weight.

[15 seconds pause]

I make healthy food and exercise choices. Relaxation is my natural strength. I am loved and light hearted. I am full of positive energy. All I need is inside of me. I befriend my body. I eat slowly. I only give my body fruits, protein, grains and nutritious foods.

[5 seconds pause]

I make healthy food and exercise choices. Relaxation is my natural strength. I am loved and light hearted. I am full of positive energy. All I need is inside of me. I befriend my body. I eat slowly. I only give my body fruits, protein, grains and nutritious foods.

[5 seconds pause]

I make healthy food and exercise choices. Relaxation is my natural strength. I am loved and light hearted. I am full of positive energy. All I need is inside of me. I befriend my body. I eat slowly. I only give my body fruits, protein, grains and nutritious foods.

[15 seconds pause]

I love how exercise made my body and mind feel. I wake up every morning refreshed and energized. I exercise my body for fun. I take time for myself. My self-care is important to me. I am taking good care of myself so I can be there for others. I pamper myself. I choose food that truly nourishes me. I speak to myself as I am a best friend or loved one.

[5 seconds pause]

I love how exercise made my body and mind feel. I wake up every morning refreshed and energized. I exercise my body for fun. I take time for myself. My self-care is important to me. I am taking good care of myself so I can be there for others. I pamper myself. I choose food that truly nourishes me. I speak to myself as I am a best friend or loved one.

[5 seconds pause]

I love how exercise made my body and mind feel. I wake up every morning refreshed and energized. I exercise my body for fun. I take time for myself. My self-care is important to me. I am taking good care of myself so I can be there for others. I pamper myself. I choose food that truly nourishes me. I speak to myself as I am a best friend or loved one.

[15 seconds pause]

It's easy for me to achieve the weight that is right for me. Nourishing my body is a priority. I keep track of success. I love being in nature walking and being active. I am free to be me. I easily let go of excess weight. I enjoy the lightness of my weight. Letting go of the past and starting over learning lesson. I love my body unconditionally. I am ready for a fresh start.

[5 seconds pause]

It's easy for me to achieve the weight that is right for me. Nourishing my body is a priority. I keep track of success. I love being in nature walking and being active. I am free to be me. I easily let go of excess weight. I enjoy the lightness of my weight. Letting go of the past and starting over learning lesson. I love my body unconditionally. I am ready for a fresh start.

[5 seconds pause]

It's easy for me to achieve the weight that is right for me. Nourishing my body is a priority. I keep track of success. I love being in nature walking and being active. I am free to be me. I easily let go of excess weight. I enjoy the lightness of my weight. Letting go of the past and starting over learning lesson. I love my body unconditionally. I am ready for a fresh start.

[15 seconds pause]

I love the taste of the healthy food. My energy is increasing a little bit more every day. I am strong and focused. I stay hydrated drink this much water I need. My immune system is strong and brilliant. I love setting and achieving goals. I eat only what I need. I like trying new fun ways to move my body. I now realize that fruits and vegetables are so good for me.

[5 seconds pause]

I love the taste of the healthy food. My energy is increasing a little bit more every day. I am strong and focused. I stay hydrated drink this much water I need. My immune system is strong and brilliant. I love setting and achieving goals. I eat only what I need. I like trying new fun ways to move my body. I now realize that fruits and vegetables are so good for me.

[5 seconds pause]

I love the taste of the healthy food. My energy is increasing a little bit more every day. I am strong and focused. I stay hydrated drink this much water I need. My immune system is strong and brilliant. I love setting and achieving goals. I eat only what I need. I like trying new fun ways to move my body. I now realize that fruits and vegetables are so good for me.

[15 seconds pause]

I can comfort myself in healthy ways. I am my own best friend. New healthy habits come easily to me. Every day I am becoming stronger. I am resilient and full of life. Change is good for me. I enjoy natural food. I am safe, I feel the safety of myself. I listen to my intuition. I approve of myself.

[5 seconds pause]

I can comfort myself in healthy ways. I am my own best friend. New healthy habits come easily to me. Every day I am becoming stronger. I am resilient and full of life. Change is good for me. I enjoy natural food. I am safe, I feel the safety of myself. I listen to my intuition. I approve of myself.

[5 seconds pause]

I can comfort myself in healthy ways. I am my own best friend. New healthy habits come easily to me. Every day I am becoming stronger. I am resilient and full of life. Change is good for me. I enjoy natural food. I am safe, I feel the safety of myself. I listen to my intuition. I approve of myself.

[15 seconds pause]

I can do anything I set mind to. I am successful managing my life. Change is good for me. I listen to my body. I give it what it need. I enjoy all types of wholesome foods. I eat only when I am hungry. I have successfully reached my ideal weight and size. I will maintain this lifestyle of health and fitness.

[5 seconds pause]

I can do anything I set mind to. I am successful managing my life. Change is good for me. I listen to my body. I give it what it need. I enjoy all types of wholesome foods. I eat only when I am hungry. I have successfully reached my ideal weight and size. I will maintain this lifestyle of health and fitness.

[5 seconds pause]

I can do anything I set mind to. I am successful managing my life. Change is good for me. I listen to my body. I give it what it need. I enjoy all types of wholesome foods. I eat only when I am hungry. I have successfully reached my ideal weight and size. I will maintain this lifestyle of health and fitness.

IV. Quit Smoking Hypnosis

7. Weight Loss Hypnosis – I (40 minutes)

This is a hypnosis meditation for weight loss. Do not listen to this audio when you are operating heavy machinery or driving. You should not be doing something that requires your attention. It is suggested to listen to this audio lying down or sitting comfortably on your bed, sofa, or a mat. This hypnosis should best be enjoyed using headphones. By the time you reach the end of this audio, you will wake up completely relaxed and reinvigorated.

So, close your eyes and let go of any thoughts that have been troubling you. This time is solely for your healing. Listen to my voice with full focus and follow my instructions. If your mind wanders during the course of the hypnosis, gently bring it back. It is the very nature of the mind to find ways to escape attention. Do not worry; this hypnosis isn't for your conscious mind. Through this hypnosis, I will be commanding your subconscious mind. Your subconscious mind is always awake and active even when your conscious mind is wandering away, is in-attentive or even asleep. So, the hypnosis will work and your subconscious mind will find ways to get you the desired weight loss results that you seek. For that, you need to simply relax. Let go of any doubts and fears. Everything is going to be alright. This hypnosis will go perfectly fine. Right now, you need to simply relax and let go of any thoughts. Loosen up your body. First I will be relaxing your physical body to make it easier for your subconscious mind to follow my instructions and act on it. The physical body relaxation will calm down your mind as well. The calmer you are the more attentive your subconscious mind is. So, all in all, you don't need to do anything at all. You simply stay relaxed. So, let's begin.

Close your eyes. Relax your mind. Relax your body. Relax your muscles and breathe in deeply through your lungs with air. Hold the breath for a moment and release.

[5 seconds pause]

Once more take in full deep breath into the chest; hold for a moment and soften your jaw and release.

[5 seconds pause]

Inhale again softly, hold here for a moment, allow your body to fully settle and exhale slowly listen to the air leaving your body as you feel your chest fall.

[5 seconds pause]

Now, as I count down from 10 with each number become more and more relax. Simply allow yourself to drift.

We begin our countdown from at ten: feeling our feet, ankles, calves, and thigh muscles, feel them relax. Allow the foundation of your whole body to melt into the spaces as you allow your legs as a gift to rejuvenate and relaxation.

[5 seconds pause]

Nine: bring your awareness to your hips. Visualize the muscles surrounding your hips, they are strong, they are healthy. They hold the root of your body all together connecting your legs to your core. With every respiration allow to sink your hips deeper into your comfortable space. Allow those muscles to simply relax.

[5 seconds pause]

Eight: bring your awareness now to your belly. Allow your belly the gift of rest and rejuvenation as your belly soften. As you come into the deep relaxation in your belly and digestive system are no longer hard at work. Imagine your belly and cells slowly winding down as your body goes into a state of deep peace. Allow your body this moment to reset from the day.

[5 seconds pause]

Seven: feel your ribcage. Feel the body into space. Focus your attention on this area as you breathe in. these ribs hug your heart and lungs with the loving embrace. They protect your organs from harm, there are here to maintain your life force. Inhale deeply visualize your ribcage; expand as your lungs filled with air as you hold here for a moment. Exhale; visualize your ribcage falling as you lungs deflate.

[5 seconds pause]

Six: you come into deeper peace as you allow your body to rest beautifully. Focus your attention to your beautiful heart. And as you visualize your heart, notice how protected and safe your heart is. It beats gently deep inside your body and it is protected by your ribcage and your lungs. As you commonly floats into the state of deep calm and peace, your heart is beating for you. It is alive and aware of your body coming into rest; it starts to slow down. Breathe in to your heart space feel your lungs expands hold the breath and exhale as you release your chest into deeper and deeper relaxation.

[5 seconds pause]

Five: bring your awareness on your shoulders and arms all the way down to your wrists. Notice where they are, notice where they rest. These are the limbs that guide and assist you towards your dreams. Visualize what good you did to your limbs and hands. Allow them to simply be as they rest for the day.

[5 seconds pause]

Four: your neck, scalp, and face relaxes a little more. Feel your jaw softens. Allow your tongue to settle and at the most peaceful place. Let go of any tension, worry or pain you hold. The worry declines, the pain slips allow them to melt away, allow them in their most natural comfortable expression.

[5 seconds pause]

Four: Shift your awareness to your nose. Become aware of its wonderful function. And allow it the ability to smell, breath and taste. However your nose is now, allowing it in its most peaceful comfort. As you slow your breathing down to deeper state of relaxation. From your nose to your ears allow the strands of your hair rest. Allow it all too simply be here now with you.

Two: notice the way your body feels, relax and lose in comfort. Notice the softness in your joints. Allow the body relaxes as it's gently releases any tension. Allow your consciousness to expand carry into deeper relaxation.

One: turn your awareness towards your thoughts. Notice thoughts which are seeking your attention. As you witness their noise chatter, give them permission to quiet and allow them place to relax. You are safe, peaceful and contend. As you take your next breath, allow the quiet rhythm to carry you deeper into your restful state of trance.

[30 seconds pause]

You find yourself inside a big auditorium. It's completely empty; just you standing at entrance of this big hall. All you can see is vacant seats all around you. It's completely dark in there. And suddenly a big-theatre-size screen in front of you lights up. And you can see your name written on the screen in bold letters. Then the screen reads, "Please, have a seat." And you find a comfortable, relaxing sofa seat next to you and you sit down. It feels so comfortable and relaxing.

[5 seconds pause]

The screen lights up again and shows all the food items that are unhealthy and not good for you. These may include carbonated drinks, highly processed food, and junk food, deeply fried and fatty food. It may also have some food items that you are allergic to. So, on the big screen, you have all the unhealthy, harmful, and bad food items. Now I want you to notice how your body feels looking at these food items.

[5 seconds pause]

You know that these items are not good for your health. Eating them may make you feel good for a moment and give your mood a temporary lift but in the long run they make you feel heavy, bloated, tired and depressed and may eventually contribute to serious illness. I am not saying that you should never have them but you need to beware of what you consume and try not to eat them. Overeating such unhealthy items is bound to make you feel guilty about yourself after a while and also make you put on extra fat in your body.

[5 seconds pause]

Now the screen changes with foods they are good for you. These are the foods which are healthy and full of protein, nutrients, and all the essential vitamins. These real foods include fresh fruits, fresh vegetables, green leafy vegetables, and whole grain, water and vegetables proteins, tofu.

[5 seconds pause]

You might realise that they now evoke a more positive response. You respect and honour your body. You know much these healthy foods will help you in reaching your goal of weight loss. And now, you feel that you have begun to like these healthy and nutritious food items.

[5 seconds pause]

Eating these foods will give you more energy and strength. You will be more productive and efficient at work. A change in diet will lead to an overall positive change in your lifestyle.

[5 seconds pause]

And you see a message from on the screen: Choose your option and you will be served. You know what you have to choose – the healthy food items. You have made a decision to lose weight and you realise how much these items will help you in achieving your goal. And soon, the you can see a table in front of you laid with healthy, nutritious food items.

[5 seconds pause]

Now you begin to serve yourself. And you choose to put only healthy food on your plate. You choose the healthy, nutritious items and put only that much quantity that you think you need to eat. You know that physical hunger is not the same as emotional hunger. Right now, you are emotionally balanced, so you can successfully gauge your hunger. You know that you will be satiated with less food. And you know that even if you eat less now, you can always eat later if you feel hungry after a while. So you judiciously put only small quantities of food on your plate.

[5 seconds pause]

You look at the plate and take a mindful breath. You can breathe in the freshness of these food items. You use your fork and knife or you can use a spoon or your hands depending on the food item you choose to eat first. You take a bite, you feel the textures in your mouth, and you chew it properly. And you can enjoy the taste now. You never knew healthy food items could taste so well because earlier you used to eat unmindfully but now you are eating consciously and savouring the food. You chew the food properly and then swallow it. You can feel the food going down the food pipe and entering your stomach. And you can sense the food healing your stomach, burning away all the fat cells. You realise that these healthy food items have the ability to heal you from the inside. Not just that they also keep you more active and alert throughout the day. And you know how much a good lifestyle means to you.

[5 seconds pause]

And you think to yourself, "Today will be the day I will turn my life around. From now onwards, I will eat only healthy and nutritious food. I will drink a lot of water and keep me hydrated. I will follow a proper exercise routine to complement my diet. I deserve the best of health and fitness and I will reach my goal through efforts and perseverance. My journey to my perfect weight starts from here."

[5 seconds pause]

Take three long and deep breaths. Inhale from the nose and exhale from the mouth.

Breathe in... And out.

[5 seconds pause]

Breathe in... And out.

[5 seconds pause]

Breathe in... And out.

[5 seconds pause]

Relax.

[5 seconds pause]

Now, I will be counting from one to ten. And when I reach ten, I want you to open your eyes and be fully aware. With each number I say, you will become more and more relaxed and more and more aware of yourself and your surroundings. Listen to my instructions and do as I command. I am now beginning with the countdown.

One: You are conscious of your existence. You are listening to my voice with full awareness. Even if you were un-attentive during the hypnosis, you have now complete awareness of each word that I say. Your subconscious mind was active and has received my messages. It is working out to find ways to bring you the desired results. So, now you can come back. Follow my voice.

Two: You can now listen to your mind's chatter. You can hear hour thoughts. The internal dialogue is audible to you. Be relaxed. Be aware. Be relaxed. Be aware. Be relaxed. Be aware.

Three: You are aware of the space you are in. You can feel your physical body. You are back in the reality now; back in the real world.

Four: You can feel the outer layer of your body. You can the texture of the clothing touching your skin.

Five: You can now notice your sense of smell. Can you smell anything peculiar? Or is it plain air that you breathe?

Six: And can you hear the noises coming from outside the room? Any noise from inside the room?

Seven: Feel your body. Feel your feet, your legs, and your hips.   Be aware of your hands and wrists and your elbows and your entire arms. Now your shoulders and neck and chin. Now bring your awareness into your entire face. Feel your eyes resting in your sockets; now your forehead and your scalp. In a moment, be aware of your entire physical body.

Eight: And you are back, back in your senses, back in the present moment. You know that anytime you open your eyes, you will be back. So you are ready now. Feel the confidence in your body. Feel the flow of energy in your body.

Nine: You are aware of the present moment, be here of the now.

Ten: Coming back completely into the physical awareness, feel your presence, feel your being. Gently open your eyes. Welcome Back!

8. Weight loss Hypnosis – II (45 minutes)

Do not listen to this audio when you are operating heavy machinery or driving. You should not be doing something that requires your attention. It is suggested to listen to this audio lying down or sitting comfortably on your bed, sofa, or a mat. This hypnosis should best be enjoyed using headphones. By the time you reach the end of this audio, you will wake up completely relaxed and reinvigorated.

[5 seconds pause]

Pay attention passively. Sometimes we tend to force ourselves to be relaxed. Don't try too hard or force yourself to relax, just allow yourself to be relaxed. Your Let go, just focus on letting go. Just vanish your mind wonder little bit, that's what it does, anything else doesn't matter, just ignore it. Gently return back to focusing your breath or your body. May be you try to force yourself to focus to hard or too many distractions in your mind?

[5 seconds pause]

Just observe that with indifference. Allow yourself to acknowledge this sensation that you feel. Any sound that you hear, any thought in your mind, just accept that. Move on and just forget about them.

[5 seconds pause]

Start with the focusing on your breath. Just observing your breath, don't try to change your breath any way, your body is breathing for you. Just breathe in and out natural and when you do release that breath, you will see you can use that breath to relax little bit more deeply. Maybe use that release of the breath, just allows yourself to become little more lose, little bit more soft in your limbs. Take a nice deep breath in, as you are ready to take breath in just fill those lungs all the way up to the top, maybe holding that breathe for a few seconds. And exhale slowly, relax just feel the wave of relaxation is running through your body. And body to become heavy.

[10 seconds pause]

Return to normal breathing.

[15 seconds pause]

Breathe in fully. And just send a huge wave of relaxation through your body. Just allow your arms, your legs, to become completely loosen up. Just let go entirely. Allow the hold of your body to become loosening. Now pay your attention to soles of your feet, it will relax your body even further. Imagine now a warm glow just spreading all over the soles of your feet; just picture that in your mind. It spreads up slowly to the rest of your body.

[5 seconds pause]

Now imagine a warm glow is spreading through your feet, imagine it is dissolving every tension from your muscles; flowing all the way to your ankles, up through your legs. See you can send that feeling up to the calves, to the shins, to the knees. Till the knees you are relax completely, imagine these muscles are turning into jelly.

[5 seconds pause]

Imagine that feeling arriving up through your thighs into your hips, both the legs completely relaxed. Just let go of every tension on your left leg and to your right leg, both the legs together.

[5 seconds pause]

Now imagine that feeling spreading up to your tummy, into your waist, up through the whole of the center of your body. Now spreading up into your chest, shoulders just fill the whole of your body. Imagine that relaxation spreading deep inside of body, into your internal organs. Send that feeling to your neck and shoulders, just imagine a color. That color is filled up your shoulders, down into the arms. Allow those arms to become loose and limp and heavy. All the way down to the very tips of your fingers.

[5 seconds pause]

Bring your awareness to your torso in a natural movement of your breath. As you focus on your breath, you may feel that the breath changing on its own. Just keep on breathing, its own pattern of breathing. Allow your body to do breathing for you all of its own. Let go of that feeling that you need to control of your breath. Let it find its own natural rhythm.

[5 seconds pause]

Notice that how relaxed you have become towards your breath. More you let go, more peaceful you become. Let go of that breathing, just let go of that effort of breathing. Your breath becomes very soft and gentle.

[5 seconds pause]

Imagine now that sense of relaxation spreading down from the base of your spine, all the way up to the back bone, to your neck. Just let that sensation flow from the back bone of your scalp down over your forehead. Relax all the muscles in your eyes and under eyes.

[5 seconds pause]

Let that glow spread into your cheeks, down into your jaw. Just send that relaxation feeling into your mouth. Just soften all the muscle on your mouth, throughout the tongue to rest flats and heavy and quiet. Just on the floor of your mouth. See if you can relax right into the root of your toe, just let it go completely. [5 seconds pause]

Now that feeling into your eyes, just notice that you relax your eyes really deeply. Just turn inwards or your eyes drift up. Back on to your lips. Just relax all the muscles of your face completely. Allow them to soften. Now notice your facial expression becoming relaxed and peaceful.

[5 seconds pause]

And this way we can relax our body. Whole body is becoming heavy and warm. Your whole body is heavy and warmed. Your right leg is becoming heavy and warm. Your right leg is becoming heavy and warm. Your right leg is now heavy and warm.

Your left leg is becoming heavy and warm. Your right leg is becoming heavy and warm. Your right leg is now heavy and warm. Your both legs are becoming heavy and warm.

[5 seconds pause]

Your left arm is becoming heavy and warm. Your left leg is becoming heavy and warm. Your left leg is heavy and warm. Your right leg is becoming heavy and warm. Your right leg is becoming heavy and warm. Your right leg is heavy and warm. Your both arms are becoming heavy and warm.

[5 seconds pause]

Your whole body is becoming heavy and warm. Your whole body is becoming heavy and warm. Your whole body is now heavy and warm. Just allow your mind to become quiet, become peaceful, allow your body to rest, to do nothing, just resting deeper, deeper into silence. You are entering a state of deep, restful trance.

[5 minutes pause]

I want you to imagine in your mind's eye your safe place. Safe place is a place where you feel the most safe and comfortable. It can be a room or spot in your house or a spot in the woods or a beach or riverside or any other place of comfort and safety. If you can't think of a place, you can create one in your mind right now. So, imagine yourself in your safe place. How do you feel?

[5 seconds pause]

How do you feel being in your safe place now? See the details, feel completely present.

[5 seconds pause]

What do you see?

[5 seconds pause]

Notice the colors in your safe place. Notice that you can control those colors. You can turn up the brightness of those colors. Making them twice as bright perhaps twice as bold or may be eventen times as bright or ten times as bold.

[5 seconds pause]

Can you listen to any sounds?

[5 seconds pause]

Can you smell any fragrances or any other peculiar odor?

[5 seconds pause]

And you roam around, making a clear picture of your safe place in your mind.

[10 seconds pause]

And on a table in the safe house, you notice a huge jug filled with clear water. And there's an empty glass placed next to it. So you help yourself and pour that clear, healthy-looking water into the glass and drink it. Feel as the water flows into your body.

[5 seconds pause]

And you feel so good and cleansed. You decide to have one more glass of water; and then one more.

[5 seconds pause]

You know how much water is good for your health. It cleanses your body, keeps you hydrated, and energises you.

[5 seconds pause]

Here in your safe place you notice now that they are two very long tales before you one on either side. One of those tables is filled with the most delicious looking foods a, vegetables and clean, clear, crisp pitchers of waters; all this beautiful, delicious looking food ripe from mother earth. Really see, feel experience, this gorgeous table and notice all the vibrant colors. Perhaps there are even some foods that you have never even seen before but they are absolutely vibrant and beautiful. Noticing this bounty of this beautiful fresh fruits, vibrant veggies, clean, clear, crisp pitchers of water just waiting for someone to pick them.

[5 seconds pause]

Now take a moment to notice the other table on the other side. This table is filled with junk food. You can notice all the junk foods, the sweets, and oily snacks. Perhaps you might have once found these unhealthy items tempting. Notice now all the colors of that table, notice that they are dull and lifeless and boring. They almost look of the same boring color. They look so dull and lifeless. You can't even imagine eating such boring-looking food.

[5 seconds pause]

Now take a moment to look back at the vibrant fruits and vegetables and see how beautifully they are filled with different colors. Beautiful deliciousness is inviting you to take a bite.

[5 seconds pause]

And turn back to the junk food table and see this ashy, dark, boring, lifeless food. In fact it's so lifeless that you see flies buzzing around landing on all of the junk food and taking bites and eating, doing lot of things that flies do flying all over this table of junk food. The flies want to take over this table because nobody wants to taste this junk food. It's just so dull and lifeless.

[5 seconds pause]

Notice now that you have a basket in your hands. In this basket is a picnic basket here designed for you, for a beautiful perfect picnic in your safe place. At this point that the food is the fuel. Go ahead and fill up your picnic basket with all of the beautiful vibrant food from the fruits and vegetables. Easily choosing the beautiful, vibrant food, in fact it is no competition to take one more glance over to the junk food table and noticing that these of flies are completely taking over. And it feels so good to chosen the vibrant food in the table. Go ahead and take few moments here taking your time to fill up your picnic basket with the most beautiful, delicious vibrant looking food.

[20 seconds pause]

And once you have done that, go ahead and find yourself sitting down on your picnic blanket. Perhaps taking out some of the delicious fruits and vegetables; picking up the most beautiful looking one, to prepare your first bite. Now take a bite of your fruit or vegetable now; feel that crisp. Wipe that juice off your chin or feeling it drips all the way down to your elbow. Just notice the fruits of your labor.

[5 seconds pause]

This vibrant, gorgeous food you have chewslowly, easily and effortlessly, in fact you chew so well with such intention in mindfulness. You chew all of the food so effortlessly.

[5 seconds pause]

As you swallow, you feel an experience that the nutrients of that food flowing down, deeper down. You can feel how good it feels to fuel your body with nutrients. Take a few moments to enjoy all that is here, and noticing with each mindful bite and with each liquid swallow, you feel more and more alight with your body and mind experience. You realize that you are fueling your body with equal nutrients that needs and wants. Now you have finished the last couple of bites of your picnic, go ahead and get up.

[5 seconds pause]

Now you stand up, walk a few steps and see before you a mirror there in your safe place. In this mirror there is magical mirror that allows you to imagine the new version of you. This is new you is in alignment with your goals. You imagine to be fitted into your favorite clothes, which you have been waiting to fit into. Whatever it is, whatever goal has brought you here today go ahead and notice this magical mirror is transforming your reflection to the perfect version of you that you desire.

[5 seconds pause]

And see that you now standing before you, easily and effortlessly. Notice the expression on your face. Take a look down at your hands. What you are wearing. Taking a nice deep breath here.taking in this transformation and seeing how easy it was to envision that transformation. Knowing that mind knows no difference between imagination and reality.

[5 seconds pause]

Now you can notice before you a door. Go ahead and walk up to the door. It's a door of transformation. As walking through the door and closing the door behind you allows you to close the door behind you on any old narratives and old stories that no longer serve you.

With your hand on your door of transformation, go ahead and open this door. And walk through this door of everlasting transformation. And feeling just how good it feels to stand through into the other side. You are feeling more comfortable, than you have ever felt. With your hand still on the everlasting transformation close the door behind you. You have closed the door behind you. You have closed the door on old narratives .you have closed the door on excuses. You have seen the new version of you. You have seen the transformed version of you.

Taking a few moments here, allowing those radiant transformative and very true statements to sink into every single cell of body now. Allow that transformation to absorb into the every cell in your body now.

[15 minutes pause]

Now, I will be counting from one to ten. And when I reach ten, I want you to open your eyes and be fully aware. This is to bring you back from the state of hypnosis to the state of normal alertness. With each number I say, you will become more and more relaxed and more and more aware of yourself and your surroundings. Open your eyes only when I reach ten and ask you to do so. The countdown will heal you and will give your subconscious mind enough time to adjust to the state of wakefulness. Listen to my instructions and do as I command. I am now beginning with the countdown.

One: You are conscious of your existence. You are listening to my voice with full awareness. Even if you were un-attentive during the hypnosis, you have now complete awareness of each word that I say. Your subconscious mind was active and has received my messages. It is working out to find ways to bring you the desired results. So, now you can come back. Follow my voice.

Two: You can now listen to your mind's chatter. You can hear hour thoughts. The internal dialogue is audible to you. Be relaxed. Be aware. Be relaxed. Be aware. Be relaxed. Be aware.

Three: You are aware of the space you are in. You can feel your physical body. You are back in the reality now; back in the real world.

Four: You can feel the outer layer of your body. You can the texture of the clothing touching your skin.

Five: You can now notice your sense of smell. Can you smell anything peculiar? Or is it plain air that you breathe?

Six: And can you hear the noises coming from outside the room? Any noise from inside the room?

Seven: Feel your body. Feel your feet, your legs, and your hips. Feel your abdomen and your chest region. Feel your entire spinal column, feel your back. Be aware of your hands and wrists and your elbows and your entire arms. Now your shoulders and neck and chin.

Now bring your awareness into your entire face. Feel your eyes resting in your sockets; now your forehead and your scalp. In a moment, be aware of your entire physical body.

Eight: And you are back, back in your senses, back in the present moment. You know that anytime you open your eyes, you will be back. So you are ready now. Feel the confidence in your body. Feel the flow of energy in your body.

Nine: You are aware of the present moment, be here of the now. This present moment is the reality. You are back. Be aware of your breathing. Be aware of the in-breath. Be aware of the out-breath. Be aware of the in-breath. Be aware of the out-breath. Very good! Be aware of the in-breath. Be aware of the out-breath.

Ten: Coming back completely into the physical awareness, feel your presence, feel your being. Bring your hands to your eyes and gently massage them. Now you return to your consciousness. Blink your eyes. Gently, very gently open your eyes. Welcome Back!

9. Weight Loss Hypnosis – III (50 minutes)

While listening to this audio, you might enter a hypnotic trance. Do not listen to when operating heavy machinery or driving. Listen to my voice with full focus and follow my instructions. If your mind wanders during the course of the hypnosis, gently bring it back. It is the very nature of the mind to find ways to escape attention. Do not worry; this hypnosis isn't for your conscious mind. Through this hypnosis, I will be commanding your subconscious mind. Your subconscious mind is always awake and active even when your conscious mind is wandering away, is in-attentive or even asleep. So, the hypnosis will work and your subconscious mind will find ways to get you the desired weight loss results that you seek. For that, you need to simply relax. Let go of any doubts and fears. Everything is going to be alright. This hypnosis will go perfectly fine. Right now, you need to simply relax and let go of any thoughts. Loosen up your body. First I will be relaxing your physical body to make it easier for your subconscious mind to follow my instructions and act on it. The physical body relaxation will calm down your mind as well. The calmer you are the more attentive your subconscious mind is. So, let's begin.

[5 seconds pause]

Scan your body beginning at the top of your head and moving down. Turn your attention to your head observe moving your attention downward to a level of your eyes, nose, chin, down to your shoulders. Noticing each area observing how your body feels. Keep scanning, gradually moving down to your body. How does your upper body feel?

[5 seconds pause]

Take note of any areas of tensions. Nearing the center of your body at the level of your stomach; how is this part of your body feeling?

[5 seconds pause]

Keep observing your physical state. Continue to scan your body moving the focus of your attention down. Reaching the level of your hips, keep observing and moving your attention down. How does this part of body feel? Notice any tension without trying to change anything.

[5 seconds pause]

Reaching the level of your knees; how does this area of your body feel? Keep scanning all the way down to your feet. Take a moment now to scan your whole body, noticing how your body feels as a whole. Where is your body the most stressful?

[5 seconds pause]

Focus intently on this one area of tension and imagine the muscles here. Let go of their hold becoming lose, become relaxed, and let the tension go. Releasing the tension bit by bit until this area relaxes.
[5 seconds pause]

Feel the tensions softening, feel the muscles as they lose them, blink them warming and relaxing as if they are melting into relaxation. Notice where your body is most relaxed. How does the relaxation feel?
[5 seconds pause]
Imagine that this relaxation is warm and tingly, moving growing, spreading to relax other parts of your body. Feel your body becoming more relaxed as the area of the relaxation grows. Allow your body to relax. Feel your shoulders relaxing. The muscle releasing there hold.
[5 seconds pause]
Your legs are still and are starting to feel heavy. Your feet are very warm, feel the warmth spreading as your legs become warmer. Your arms are getting heavier, feel yourself sinking into the surface you are lying on. Sinking deeper, deeper, your whole body is feeling very heavy. Feel the warmth in your hands growing warmer and warmer, spreading up to your arms.
[5 seconds pause]
Your hands and arms are very heavy. Notice the feeling of coolness in your forehead, calm, cool and relaxed, and free from tension. Imagine that the tension in your body is flowing out through your fingers and toes, draining away. With each breath you can feel the tension leaving right out your finger tips and right out your toes. Feel the tension leaving your body, draining away.
[5 seconds pause]
Let your mind drift away for a moment. Just relaxing not needing to focus or think just drifting as the tension used to drain way and your body relaxes. Imagine a feeling of warmth and relaxation starting in your hands and feet. Your hands and feet are melting and becoming soft, getting softer and more relaxed. The warmth spreads around your body from your hands up your arms. Feel your arms melting, softening. It is a pleasant feeling, so relaxing. Feel the warmth as it continue up from your feet and your legs.
[5 seconds pause]
Notice your legs softening as if they are melting to relax state. Feel the core of your body as the warmth coming through your arms and legs meets your stomach. Feel your core relaxing, melting. Imagine that your whole body is very soft and melted into a relaxation.
[5 seconds pause]

Floating, relaxing, it's ok to just relax now. Letting your mind drift off, drifting to relaxation. Your body is like a feather now, floating down to the peaceful land. Feel your body drifting back and forth down and down. There are no words you need to focus on, just be calm. Enjoy the relaxation now.

[10 minutes pause]

And in this state of trance, you are going deeper and deeper. In this state of pure trance, you can learn anything, you can grow exponentially, and you can form new habits and change the old ones. Your subconscious is fully absorbing all the commands now. It will retain everything. All the information, all the instructions, and all the guidance will be completely adhered to. In this state of pure trance, there are no filters. Everything is absorbed completely. It is the best state to break old patterns of thoughts or form new habits. That's why I have brought you here – to rewire the way you think about food; to recondition your mind about health and fitness. Everything single word that I say now will be retained. Every message will be absorbed without any filtration. And there's no limit to how much your subconscious mind can take in.

Your subconscious is like a sponge. This sponge soaks up all information, all the information which does you good and let you grows. In this sponge can excess all the information at any time whenever you need it. Nothing gets lost. You relax deeper and deeper and deeper.

[5 seconds pause]

And you are so deep in this trance right now that you can't tell if you are already asleep or are still awake. You are now in the deepest state of relaxation. In this state everything is possible. Today, you are going to learn so many new things. But before that you will have to unlearn. You will have to unlearn the habits that have been harming. You tried a lot to change those harmful habits earlier but could not do so. But you can do that now.

[5 seconds pause]

This is the time to unlearn and throw away every negative habit, every negative thought pattern that has been hindering your progress in life. You deserve so much. But your bad habits always came in the way. No more! You are about to change forever – you are going to change for the better. You will open your mind to new experiences and new information. You will replace the words I can't with I can. Your subconscious will is open to new learn new things. Your subconscious will replace the unhealthy with healthy ways of thinking in your mind. From now on, your mind will be alerted each time you yield to old impulses. You will no longer be the slave to your past. It is time to rewrite your life and your destiny.

[5 seconds pause]

Your subconscious will change the way you think and react. Your mind will be alerted if you are harsh and unfair to yourself. Your subconscious will send you a signal to stop from moment before you react in the same old way. You will no longer be the prisoner of your habits. Your subconscious will send you a signal to stop. Your subconscious will send you a signal to stop for a moment before you react in the same old way. And when you stop you will get the choice. You will make the right choice. You will make use of all the possibilities open to you. You will know about the power of these possibilities of the future.

[5 seconds pause]

When you are in such a level of awareness, the entire universe gets into action to get you to reach your goals. And this will show in the results. You are on path to transformation. You will no longer react in similar fashion. Earlier, you used to react automatically, almost that you are an auto pilot. You reacted to the impulse only at these moments in time. You filled and presumed need impulse but you have a choice at all time. You have a choice. When this impulse arises keeps it inside, pause, wait and choose, pause, wait and choose. Go from subconscious action to conscious action. You have a choice at all times. You have this choice whenever the impulse arises. And you will make the full use of these choices now.

[5 seconds pause]

You will do what's right for you. From subconscious action to conscious action from auto pilot to decision and if you make this choice you have a profound influence on your mind. This will then have a profound effect on your body, your soul, and your mind. You have decided to get the control back over your life.

[5 seconds pause]

You are about to change the way you view your food and diet. You are going to make the use of your power to choose. And then you can choose, you can choose to eat anything unhealthy or something healthy. You can choose between healthy and unhealthy. You have this choice. You see yourself reflected in this decision from now on. You will see how you choose; you look at all the possibilities. You pause, wait and choose. This is how you train your subconscious. You decide to choose.

[5 seconds pause]

You prefer to drink fresh water over all other carbonated drinks. You realize the importance of water. Water is one of the five elements that form the universe. It is essential for your survival and growth. So, you have decided that from now on you will take in water in its purest form. Water will keep you alive; it will keep you healthy. You realize that water is life and it must not be consumed after mixing harmful chemicals in it. From now on, you will consume only fresh water. This water give nourish you with all the essential nutrients it contains. From now on, you will drink more and more water. You will detoxify your body with this unique and powerful element. It helps your skin to detoxify and achieve the healthy color. Water moves through your entire body and cleanses every single cell. You realize the infinite potential of the element of water.

[5 seconds pause]

You will want to drink 10 more glasses of water per day. Your body will take over your thought of your mind crystal clear. Like water as its source, you will eat and drink what truly nourishes you.

[5 seconds pause]

You become what you eat. So, if you supply your body with this healthy fuel, it will cleanse your body and your mind will also receive clarity and purity. You will them become a fish in water which follows its course and remains there. Until its body, mind and soul have reached their destination. Clarity, focus and choice are within you. Self-confidence is within you, lightness is within you. This high frequency is within you, pause, wait and choose. Satisfied and light and free. The frequency of your mind, body, soul will automatically increase. Food is light energy; your body stores this light energy and transforms this food into thoughts. You will have energy for truly important things. You will lose weight. You will achieve your focus. You have time for people that you truly love. You will do all the things you like doing very often. You are no longer willing to sacrifice. All this things do to your weight, where you lack of self-consciousness.

[5 seconds pause]

And in the future whenever you feel the impulse to drink or to eat something unhealthy, pause, wait and choose. Pause, wait and choose.

[5 seconds pause]

Pause, wait and choose. You will advance on this path every day. Pause, wait and choose. You have this choice at every impulse. You enter the high frequency pause, wait and choose. You can decide the time and again with this decision you set yourself free from the past. You will now no longer choose food, which constricts your body or makes it heavy. You avoid food which makes you tired, Heavy and slow. You will avoid food which makes you sluggish. You will consume food which supplies you with light energy. You will enter this light high frequency energy with each individual decision. This will precisely change your craving. Healthy eating will guide you into the light energy. You will experience it every day. You will always, always choose this light energy, choose creation, choose choice, choose new things, and choose healthy things. Pause, wait and choose.

[20 seconds pause]

And whenever you have the choice, you use the stairs instead of lifts. Your movement is freedom. Movement is letting go. Movement is light energy; movement becomes a game for you. And if the impulse arises, you decide for health. Your subconscious will now become highly creative; it will show you how you can do good to your body. It will reveal to you how you can do good to your body.

[5 seconds pause]

Your mind becomes a single self-defending element and instrument that is good for your body. There is now no room left for the old impulses. Pause, wait and choose. With those all self-ingest thoughts gather peace your subconscious mind with auto reunion with every impulse. It was strongly remind you that you now thing other way. It will remind you that always have a choice to obey and impulse what it let it go. Just let it go. You will continue with old or create something new.

[5 seconds pause]

You have the strength to create your own path. You can simply block out any negativity around you. You can block out all of all this negativity with love and all of these people who don't stand by you; possibly friend or people at work. The negative things which clog up mind so often. And you can decide to spend less time with negative people. There sheer power inside you. You except that there is nothing wrong with you no matter how much you weigh. You realize you are now forging your own path. From now on you will lose weight for yourself only. Now on you will lose weight for you, yourself only.

[5 minutes pause]

From now on, you will lead a new life. A life that is full of health and vitality. Now I as count backwards from Five to zero, you will become more and more aware with each count. And when I reach zero, you will gently open your eyes.

Five, Four, Three, Two, One, and Zero. Gently open your eyes.

10. Weight Loss Hypnosis – IV (60 minutes)

Do not listen to this audio when you are operating heavy machinery or driving. You should not be doing something that requires your attention. It is suggested to listen to this audio lying down or sitting comfortably on your bed, sofa, or a mat. This hypnosis should best be enjoyed using headphones. By the time you reach the end of this audio, you will wake up completely relaxed and reinvigorated.

So, close your eyes and let go of any thoughts that have been troubling you. This time is solely for your healing. Listen to my voice with full focus and follow my instructions. If your mind wanders during the course of the hypnosis, gently bring it back. It is the very nature of the mind to find ways to escape attention. Do not worry; this hypnosis isn't for your conscious mind. Through this hypnosis, I will be commanding your subconscious mind. Your subconscious mind is always awake and active even when the conscious mind is wandering away, is in-attentive or even asleep. So, the hypnosis will work and your subconscious mind will find ways to get you the desired weight loss results that you seek. For that, you need to simply relax.

[5 seconds pause]

Let go of any doubts and fears. Everything is going to be alright. This hypnosis will go perfectly fine. Right now, you need to simply relax and let go of any thoughts. Loosen up your body. First I will be relaxing your physical body to make it easier for your subconscious mind to follow my instructions and act on it. The physical body relaxation will calm down your mind as well. The calmer you are the more attentive your subconscious mind is. So, all in all, you don't need to do anything at all. You simply stay relaxed. So, let's begin.

Take three deep breaths. Breathing into the nose and out through the mouth. Just also come into the body. Start to feel sensation either on your chest, your belly, your shoulders of your breath, been through your body. Start to feel the weight of your legs or your arms, just the heaviness of your body; downward to the gravity.

[5 seconds pause]

Let's spread the simple grounding cord that something that connects your hips, buttocks, hip bones. Then connect that part of your body into the earth. Now each out breath, you just allow tension, mental formation, thoughts, conceptions, judgments, worries, body aches and pains, let all that go. As plenty of time, during the rest of your day to problem solve, plan. To just allow gravity and that familiar sensation to being pulled the earth. Just use that to your advantage, using that force of gravity to release negativity, anything that's not serving you today.

[5 seconds pause]

Now you will go through your body parts. Part by part and only instruction is to bring your awareness to that body part. Feel into that body part and then use your grounding cord and your exhale to release any tension anything that might be stuck, any old thing. We stuff so many things in our bodies, beliefs, traumas, joy, so just anything that's not serving you in that body part. We are just going to release to that grounding cord. We are just resetting in this present moment, in the present moment we have everything we need. So we are just bringing our energy back to ourselves away from old stories, away from the past or the future.

[5 seconds pause]

Bring your awareness to the crown of our head, the scalp, and top of our head. Can you just breathe in into that body part? Allow tensions, tightness our goal is just to relax the body as much as possible still remaining awake and alert and upright. Move your awareness into our forehead, eyebrows, space between our eyebrows move down to our eyes, eye sockets, eye lids, underneath the eyes, behind the eyes.

[5 seconds pause]

Cleanse your body and your spirit for yourself but also for everyone you going to come in contact with. The act of meditation is very generous act. Prominent to your temples or the side of your face, your cheeks, jaw bone, open of your jaw bones, can you even kind of pop your ears, release tensions or if behind sort of at the back of your jaws, connects to your skull, the back of your head, your mouth, your tongue, your hips. The relaxation is taking you into a deeper level of trance and healing.

[5 seconds pause]

Move energy through the body, down into your neck, right at the base of your head, down to your neck, down to your spine. Your head around that feels supportive and gentle. No effort in here, remember that grounding cord is doing all the work, gravity, earth. With each deep breath just letting your body unwind bit by bit.

[5 seconds pause]

Moving into the high chest, your left collar bone, your left shoulder, your left shoulder blade and together like high back on the left side. Your left armpit, your left bicep, triceps, your left elbow, your forearm, your left wrist, your left hand, your left palm, your left thumb, pointer, middle, ring, pinky, your entire left arm. The relaxation is taking you into a deeper level of trance and healing.

[5 seconds pause]

Your right collar bone, your right shoulder, right shoulder blade and right upper back, your right side, your right armpit, your right bicep and triceps, your right elbow, your right forearm, your right wrist, your entire right hand, your right palm, your right thumb, pointer, middle, ring, pinky. The relaxation is taking you into a deeper level of trance and healing.

[5 seconds pause]

Your entire right arm, again just let gravity tug at your bones, at your flesh. Merely attention you need to hold is that you're bringing your body and energy into present time. And you are letting go of what doesn't serve you. Move the awareness into your beautiful and tender heart space; the entire upper chest and torso.

[5 seconds pause]

Feel any tension, any disease, discomfort, feel your breath that part of your body. Shift your awareness down into your abdomen, into your stomach, your intestine and all the organs that work so hard. They are doing such a good job for keeping you healthy.

[5 seconds pause]

Shift the awareness into your navel, your creative home space, your pelvis, and your buttocks. Check to see that your grounding cord is set, cord of light or whatever it is. With exhalation you are releasing anything that doesn't serve you. Go back to the upper back, mid back, lower back and the bump. Just allow your entire being to be supported and held, cleansed.

[5 seconds pause]

Gently move your attention to your left thigh, buttocks, the hamstrings, to your left knee, shin and calf, left ankle, left top of foot, left bottom of foot, big toes, second toe, third, fourth, and fifth toe, all the toes, the whole left foot, whole left leg. To your right thigh, hamstring, right knee, to your right calf and shin, to your right ankle, right of foot , right bottom of foot, right big toes, second toe, third, fourth, and fifth toe, all the toes, the whole right foot, whole right leg. Now feel the relaxation fill the entire body. The relaxation is taking you into a deeper level of trance and healing.

[5 seconds pause]

Now, I want you to bring your awareness now to the interior of your body. Just check in sort of toddle your awareness, into the heart , into the chest, around the jaw, down through your legs, around the aware the exterior of the body perhaps sensation of the air, your face, temperature of the air as you breathe through into your nose feel the air, sensation of ups and backs of your hands. Feeling of your palm on your body, may be feel the sensation of the cloth on your legs. These instructions will stay in your body. Some sensations will be there, they could be the feeling of the breath in your belly, in your chest. Or it could be the temperature of the air as you inhale. Whatever it is, whatever sensation that you choose, will stay with that sensation. Feel your presence. Stay with your presence for a while.

[15 minutes pause]

Today is a new day, a new beginning. Let today be the day your life changes for the good. Let today be the day you start feeling proud of yourself.

Take three deep breaths. Breathe in and breathe out. Breathe in and breathe out. Breathe in and breathe out.

Very good; now relax.

I am now in conversation with your subconscious mind. Your subconscious mind is in charge of your eating habits. It governs your resistance to unhealthy and oily food. It decides how much to push you to go for a physical exercise. So I will now be commanding your subconscious mind to look for ways to make you slim and healthy. It will be entirely upon your subconscious mind how it achieves the goal of weight loss and transformation. Because it knows your body, it knows what will work for you and what won't. May be you have been forcing yourself into an exercise regime that does suit your body type or maybe you been doing diets that did more harm than good to your body. So, I will let your subconscious mind decide.

[5 seconds pause]

From now on, you will do physical exercise because it is important for your good health but you will do it the best way possible. And this will translate into a more healthy physical body, mental energy and emotional strength. And the benefits of having a healthier physical body, mental energy and emotional strength will expand more and more as the time passes.

[5 seconds pause]

From now on, you will exercise the way your intuition guides you to and there will be no need to discipline yourself because your sub conscious will take care of doing what it has to do without any changes that need to happen for you.

[5 seconds pause]

I am now commanding your subconscious mind to reach the part of you that is in charge of controlling your eating habits, bouncing the weight of your body. You know deep inside that the mind has the ability to control by means of switches that turned on and off that you have controlled to change level as you please. Because deep down you know that you have the power to control over your weight and what you feed your body and the amount of food you give your body. Deep down you also know that is not your stomach and your appetite that is in charge of the controlling the amount of food but you given because the truth is that in your mind you have control and power. We can take it benefit of this moment to create in this part of your sub conscious new eating habits. And create new goals for the near future. For this I am going to ask you visualize in your mind, the body you like to have. You can even remember a moment of your past in which you are at your ideal weight, or you can also create a new image the ideal body for you.

[5 seconds pause]

Visualise your ideal self as clearly as possible. Imagine your thin arms and feel your clothes on your thin body and imagine how your stomach feels, your ideal weight. We are going to taste, what the healthy food you are going eat and taste. So imagine savouring that food you know help you achieve your ideal weight and imagine feeling satisfied with the necessary portion to keep your body healthy and alive. Can you smell what that food smells like can you feel the desire to eat healthy? And only what is necessary to keep your body healthy and happy. What does it smell like?

[5 seconds pause]

And imagine what the people around you are going to say, they see your body at your ideal weight. Can you feel that how much confidence and joy you feel when having a healthy body at its ideal weight? Imagine already achieving that ideal weight. And imagine what emotions are in your body?

[5 seconds pause]

From now on it is the fact that the less you eat, the happier you will feel. That the less you eat now, the more you smile and more you feel energetic. The less you eat now; you will look better and feel better. The less you eat now, you will feel more relaxed. That the less you eat, you feel more motivated to work on your goals and to work on your dreams. Less you eat; you know you are creating a healthier body with more energy.

[5 seconds pause]

You also know that the body you want is already there inside of you. And by creating this image we are simply giving your body the opportunity to allow yourself to feel good. You also know that every day your actions are creating patterns and habits. That strengthens you and gives you more life. And you eat enough to be well, to keep your body fit and energetic. This fact is reinforced day by day with your decisions and your actions because you know that you should be healthier and stronger fit physically and mentally. And you know that movement is good for you, makes you want to move your body and listen to your body when its need water.

[5 seconds pause]

You can keep a hydrating body because as you always listen to your body telling you how much food it really needs and how much water it really needs. You know that eating what you need also means showing your food and eating slowly to save each bite of the food. Deep down you also know that things your body doesn't need to eat and you notice you feel less wanted to eat those things but don't help you be your ideal body and weight. And you know that eating healthy is only what is necessary no more than what's necessary and you know that eating healthy is only eat what is necessary and not more than necessary. You know eating healthy is eating things that are alive, such as plants, grains, or proteins and the things that are really nutritious. You continue to do what is necessary to maintain a healthy body and notice how your body is feeling incredible machine that has the capacity to module itself. Do you liking and then you can create this new habit. Do you liking and order to get a body of your dream.

[5 seconds pause]

In this moment your energies are going to transform. You feel exactly how you like to feel. So you can dress exactly you like to dress. And you can already see yourself happy with your body as you like. And you can see yourself moving your body more and more every day because you feel better. You feel healthier and fit and this makes you do more things to be more alive. You feel like you really want to work on your dreams more. You can feel this energy spreading throughout your body. This version of you is everything you want it. And you can even imagine seeing yourself at your ideal weight. Imagine as if it already happening. Imagine that you are already attained your ideal weight and feel your body at that weight. Your metabolism is already working faster; they burn all that unnecessary fat from your body as you already feel more positive and more motivated.

[5 seconds pause]

Feeling more satisfied now that something good is happening right now. Enjoying this moment because you know that is already more self-love and you know that you like to be with yourself because you accept yourself more and more every day. And you that there is no one else like you. You are unique. You are learning more and more every day to accept yourself more in a deeper level. And deep down you that you deserve better life. And you treat yourself better every day. That same love you give to everyone. You starting to give yourself love even more. Because you know that there is no one else is like you. Yourself love is getting more day by day. Your body will act accordingly to how you feel and how you look. The more you love your body the less poison you are going to give. You are going to be in charge of your body.

[5 seconds pause]

Now, I will be counting from one to ten. And when I reach ten, I want you to open your eyes and be fully aware. This is to bring you back from the state of hypnosis to the state of normal alertness. With each number I say, you will become more and more relaxed and more and more aware of yourself and your surroundings. Open your eyes only when I reach ten and ask you to do so. The countdown will heal you and will give your subconscious mind enough time to adjust to the state of wakefulness. Listen to my instructions and do as I command. I am now beginning with the countdown.

[5 seconds pause]

One: You are conscious of your existence. You are listening to my voice with full awareness. Even if you were un-attentive during the hypnosis, you have now complete awareness of each word that I say. Your subconscious mind was active and has received my messages. It is working out to find ways to bring you the desired results. So, now you can come back. Follow my voice.

Two: You can now listen to your mind's chatter. You can hear hour thoughts. The internal dialogue is audible to you. Be relaxed. Be aware. Be relaxed. Be aware. Be relaxed. Be aware.

Three: You are aware of the space you are in. You can feel your physical body. You are back in the reality now; back in the real world.

Four: You can feel the outer layer of your body. You can the texture of the clothing touching your skin.

Five: You can now notice your sense of smell. Can you smell anything peculiar? Or is it plain air that you breathe?

Six: And can you hear the noises coming from outside or inside the room?

Seven: Feel your body. Feel your feet, your legs, and your hips. Feel your abdomen and your chest region. Feel your entire spinal column, feel your back. Be aware of your hands and wrists and your elbows and your entire arms. Now your shoulders and neck and chin. Now bring your awareness into your entire face. Feel your eyes resting in your sockets; now your forehead and your scalp. In a moment, be aware of your entire physical body.

Eight: And you are back, back in your senses, back in the present moment. You know that anytime you open your eyes, you will be back. So you are ready now. Feel the confidence in your body. Feel the flow of energy in your body.

Nine: You are aware of the present moment, be here of the now. This present moment is the reality. You are back. Be aware of your breathing. Be aware of the in-breath. Be aware of the out-breath. Be aware of the in-breath. Be aware of the out-breath. Very good! Be aware of the in-breath. Be aware of the out-breath.

Ten: Coming back completely into the physical awareness, feel your presence, feel your being. Bring your hands to your eyes and gently massage them. Now you return to your consciousness. Blink your eyes. Gently, very gently open your eyes. Welcome Back!

11. Weight Loss Hypnosis (Before Sleep) – I (60 minutes)

I am now talking to your subconscious mind. You don't need to understand everything that I say because the way your subconscious mind operates and understands things is different than the ways your conscious mind do so. You don't need to try to make sense out of these things. Just listen. And even if you fall asleep, it doesn't matter either. Your subconscious mind will continue to listen to commands. So, allow yourself to relax a bit deeper now. I am counting from one to ten. Let each number make you a bit more relaxed. 1… 2… 3… 4… 5… 6… 7… 8… 9… and 10… relax, completely relax.

[5 seconds pause]

Prepare for relaxation now. Close your eyes. Spread your awareness to your entire physical body. And become aware to the large group of muscles in the arms and legs.

[5 seconds pause]

Now spread the awareness to the abdomen and chest, the shoulders, neck, and face. Now feel the awareness in all the muscles of your face, the muscles surrounding your mouth and cheeks and tongue, the muscles surrounding your eyes and forehead. Relaxation is important to calm your mind down. So whenever you find that your mind has wandered, bring it back to my voice and continue to enjoy this relaxation practice.

[5 seconds pause]

And now become aware to the muscles involved in the act of breathing. Absorb the movements of the muscles of respiration in the abdomen. There is only this present moment and this current breath. Allow the belly to become supple as you passively watch it rise and fall. As the belly rises and falls with each respiration you can feel the sensation of warmth expands the navel, spreading and expanding warmth.

[5 seconds pause]

And now bring your awareness to the expanding warmth within the right hand, lower arm, upper arm, and shoulder. This body relaxation practice is a very important part of this hypnosis as it is taking you into deeper and deeper levels of the hypnotic trance. The more your body relaxes, the more ably your subconscious mind receives my command and charts out different ways to act on them. So, continuing with this relaxation now. The right side of the torso, upper leg, lowers leg, and the foot. Now feel the relaxation in the entire right side of the body.

[5 seconds pause]

And now experience soothing warmth, spreading through the left hand to the lower arm, upper arm and shoulder. The left side of the torso, upper leg, lowers leg, and the foot. The whole left side of the body. Become aware of the whole right leg, the whole left leg, and both legs together.

[5 seconds pause]

Now feel it in the whole right arm, whole left arm, both arms together. The relaxation is taking you into a deeper level of trance and healing. The whole front side of the body, back side of the body, shoulders, neck and head. The whole body together, the whole body.

[5 seconds pause]

Now bring your awareness to the points of contacts where your body meets the surface beneath you. Feel the heaviness of your body sinking down, deeper and even deeper, surrendering to the force of gravity and the heaviness of your body. And if your mind wanders into its own world of thoughts, gently bring it back to this body scan. And again become aware to the breath at the belly and slow deep breathing.

[5 seconds pause]

Possibly witness the soothing wave like flow of each inhalation and exhalation, rising from the navel up to the base of the neck during the inhalation and back down to the navel with the exhalation.

[5 seconds pause]

Feel the soothing wave like flow of the natural breath. Relaxation is important to calm your mind down. So whenever you find that your mind has wandered, bring it back to my voice and continue to enjoy this relaxation practice. And again bring your awareness to the right hand and feel the steadiness and stillness of the right hand. The right hand thumb, second finger, third, fourth and fifth finger, Palm of the hand, back of the hand, the right wrist, lower arm, elbow, upper arm, and shoulder, the armpit, right waist, and hip.

[5 seconds pause]

The upper thigh, back of the thigh, right knee cap, back of the knee, right shin, calf muscles, ankle, heel, and sole. This body relaxation practice is a very important part of this hypnosis as it is taking you into deeper and deeper levels of the hypnotic trance. The more your body relaxes, the more ably your subconscious mind receives my command and charts out different ways to act on them. So, continuing with this relaxation now. The top of the right foot, right big toe, second, third, fourth and fifth toe. The whole right side of the body, Steady and still.

[5 seconds pause]

And now develop awareness to the steadiness of the left hand; the left hand thumb, second finger, third, fourth and fifth finger. The palms of the hand, back of the hand, the left wrist, lower arm, elbow, upper arm, and shoulder. The armpit, left waist, hip, upper thigh, back of the thigh, left knee cap, back of the knee, left shin, calf muscle, ankle, heel and sole.

[5 seconds pause]

The top of the left foot left big toe, second, third, fourth, and fifth toe. The whole left side of the body steady and still. The relaxation is taking you into a deeper level of trance and healing. Become aware to the crown of your head. Forehead, right eyebrow, left eyebrow, the center of the brows, right eyelid, left eyelid, right eye, left eye, right ear, left ear, and the nose. the top of the nose, upper lip, lower lip, right cheek, left cheek, and the chin, throat, the pit of the throat, right collar bone, left collar bone, right chest muscle, left chest muscle and the abdomen. And if your mind wanders into its own world of thoughts, gently bring it back to this body scan. Navel, lower abdomen, whole right leg, whole left leg, both legs together, the whole right arm, whole left arm, both arms together, the front side of the torso, abdomen and chest.

[5 seconds pause]

Bring your awareness to the back side of the torso, buttocks, spinal cord and the shoulder blades. Both the front and back sides of the torso together. The shoulders, neck, and face. Relaxation is important to calm your mind down. So whenever you find that your mind has wandered, bring it back to my voice and continue to enjoy this relaxation practice. Now bring your awareness to all the muscles of the face together. The right-side of the head, left side of the head, the back of the head and the crown, the crown of your head, your whole head together.

[5 seconds pause]

Your whole body, you whole body from the top of your head to the tips of your fingers and toes. Total body awareness. And the natural breath observes the spontaneous and out flow of the natural breath.

[5 seconds pause]

And bring your awareness to the sensation of sound. Remain witness, listening to the quality of each and every sound as you have never heard that before. Listen to the silence between and surrounding and resound. This body relaxation practice is a very important part of this hypnosis as it is taking you into deeper and deeper levels of the hypnotic trance. The more your body relaxes, the more ably your subconscious mind receives my command and charts out different ways to act on them. So, continuing with this relaxation now. Become aware of the silence of your mind. Prefer listening to mental silence as you can still the mind to listen you can experience the inner peace of silence.

[5 seconds pause]

Observe all external and internal sounds of the senses and the mind. Remain a passive witness to all sounds and thoughts. Merely becoming a witness; observing all sounds and thoughts with detachment. The relaxation is taking you into a deeper level of trance and healing. Now become aware to the heaviness of the right hand. Heaviness spreading from the right hand thumb to the second finger, third, fourth, fifth finger, palm of the hand, back of the hand, wrist, lower arm , elbow, upper arm, shoulder, armpit, waist, hip, right thigh, kneecap, calf muscle, ankle, heel, sole, top of the foot, right big toe, second, third, fourth, and fifth toe.

[5 seconds pause]

You may now feel the whole right side of the body heavy. And if your mind wanders into its own world of thoughts, gently bring it back to this body scan. Feel the heaviness of the left hand. Heaviness spreading on the left hand thumb to the second finger, third, fourth, fifth finger, palm of hand , back of the hand, wrist, lower arm, elbow, upper arm, shoulder, armpit, waist, hip, the left thigh, kneecap, calf muscle, ankle, heel, sole, top of the foot, left big toe, second, third, fourth, and fifth toe.

[5 seconds pause]

Bring the awareness to whole left side of the body. Relaxation is important to calm your mind down. So whenever you find that your mind has wandered, bring it back to my voice and continue to enjoy this relaxation practice. Again go to the right toes, right big toe, second, third, fourth and fifth toe.

[5 seconds pause]

Top of the right foot, the sole, heel, ankle, calf muscle, kneecap, thigh, hip, waist, armpit, right shoulder, upper arm, elbow, lower am, wrist, back of the right hand, palm of the hand, right thumb, second finger, third, fourth and fifth finger. This body relaxation practice is a very important part of this hypnosis as it is taking you into deeper and deeper levels of the hypnotic trance. The more your body relaxes, the more ably your subconscious mind receives my command and charts out different ways to act on them. So, continuing with this relaxation now.

[5 seconds pause]

Go to the left toe, left big toe, second toe, third, fourth, fifth, top of the foot, sole, heel, ankle, calf muscle, kneecap, the left thigh, hip, waist, armpit, left shoulder, upper arm, elbow, lower arm, wrist, back of the hand, palm of the hand, left thumb, second finger, third, fourth and fifth finger. The relaxation is taking you into a deeper level of trance and healing. Bring your awareness to the back of the head.

[5 seconds pause]

Feel the point of contact between the back of the head and the surface beneath you. The right shoulder blade, left shoulder blade, the whole spinal column, right hip, left hip, right buttock, left buttock, back of the right thigh, back of the left thigh, back of the right knee, back of the left knee.

[5 seconds pause]

Right calf muscle, left calf muscle, right ankle, left ankle, right heel and the left heel. And if your mind wanders into its own world of thoughts, gently bring it back to this body scan.

The right foot, the left foot, right heel, left heel, right ankle, left ankle, right calf muscle, left calf muscle, back of the right knee, back of the left knee, back of the right thigh, back of the left thigh, right buttock, left buttock, right hip, left hip. Relaxation is important to calm your mind down. So whenever you find that your mind has wandered, bring it back to my voice and continue to enjoy this relaxation practice.

[5 seconds pause]

The whole spinal column, right shoulder blade, left shoulder blade, the back of the head, the top of the head, the forehead, right eyebrow, left eyebrow, the space between the eyebrows, right eyelid, left eyelid, right eye, left eye, right ear, left ear.

[5 seconds pause]

Right nostril, left nostril, right cheek, left cheek, upper lip, lower lip, the chin, throat, right collar bone, left collar bone, right chest, left chest, the abdomen, navel, lower abdomen, right thigh, left thigh, right knee, left knee, right shin, left shin, right ankle, left ankle, top of the right foot, top of the left foot, right toes, left toes. This body relaxation practice is a very important part of this hypnosis as it is taking you into deeper and deeper levels of the hypnotic trance. The more your body relaxes, the more ably your subconscious mind receives my command and charts out different ways to act on them. So, continuing with this relaxation now.

[5 seconds pause]

Top of the right foot, top of the left foot, right ankle, left ankle, right shin, left shin, right kneecap, left kneecap, right thigh, left thigh, lower abdomen, navel, upper abdomen, right chest muscle, left chest muscle, right collar bone, left collar bone, the throat , chin, lower lip, upper lip, right cheek, left cheek, right nostril, left nostril, right eye, left eye, right eyelid, left eyelid, right eyebrow, left eyebrow, top of the head.

[5 seconds pause]

The relaxation is taking you into a deeper level of trance and healing. The whole right leg, the whole left leg, both legs together. Feel the whole Right arm, whole left arm, both arms together.

[5 seconds pause]

Now feel the whole of the front, whole of the back, the whole head, and the whole body together. And if your mind wanders into its own world of thoughts, gently bring it back to this body scan. Visualize the whole body. See a mental image of your entire body from head to toe.

[5 seconds pause]

The whole body and feel the needing points between your body and the bed. Feel the bed holding you firmly. See your body as if you are looking at it from outside. Look on your body as an object, a reflection in an imaginary mirror. Have an awareness of your body as an object. And now listen to the natural quiet breath. Become aware to the soft sound of the breath at the nostril and nasal passages. Listen to the soothing sounds of your breath. Maintain a gentle focus in your breath – the in-breath and the out-breath.

[2 minutes pause]

You have made a decision to lose weight. You have made a decision to change the shape of your physical body. You have made a decision to look more fit, lean, and more attractive. You have made a decision to get back the control back over your body, your health, your weight, your shape and size, and your future. And your subconscious mind knows how exactly to manifest your thoughts into reality. It knows that changing the shape of the body and maintaining that ideal shape requires constant hard work. Your subconscious mind will prepare you mentally and physically for the road ahead so that you don't feel tired too early and rebuild your stamina.

[5 seconds pause]

You might remember an occasion when you had a great exercise session, a perfect run, a fulfilling cycling or swimming session. Do you remember that feeling that you had after that session of physical activity? You must have felt so much alive and full of energy because your brain rewards you and your body secretes some wonderful chemicals that make you feel good.

[5 seconds pause]

Bring that beautiful feeling in your body now, feel as if you have just completed a long and testing run or a hard session in your gym or swimming pool, or you have just returned from your cycling round. Bring that feeling of achievement and contentment within you. Feel the feeling.

[20 seconds pause]

You must have noticed how good you feel now. By just imagining that feeling of exercise, your mind rewards you with good feelings. Now, I am going to command your subconscious mind to find ways to make you get into those physical activities as often as possible. I am commanding your subconscious mind to get you rid of your excuses and unhealthy habits of procrastination to get you out of your comfort zone. Your subconscious mind knows how to do that. Progress begins when you step out of your comfort zone; you need to run the extra mile to lose that extra weight.

[5 seconds pause]

You know yourself inside out. You know what you are capable of doing and achieving. You know how and from where to start. All you need to is a push to do a little more. You can walk a little more. You can jog or run a little more. You can cycle a little more. You can swim a little more.

[5 seconds pause]

And you choose the exercises that you love to do so that the physical activities leading to your rapid and extreme weight loss are full of fun. And you now look forward to your exercise sessions. You never knew that burning fat could be so much fun. You realize that as you tread on the path to weight loss, good things are happening to you. You are finding the right people, the right company for your exercise sessions. Now, you wait for the time to come so that you can go out and exercise. Losing weight has now become fun.

[5 seconds pause]

You may be surprised that how far you have progressed. You enjoying moving and stretching and exercising more than ever. As you spend more energy by move more and stretching and exercising, you are rewarded with more energy. As you build up your energy and stamina, you feel better and better and as you feel better and better you are able to do a little more. And the change in your body, your physique is quite visible. You have lost the extra fat from your body. Your physique has begun to trim down as you become slimmer.

[5 seconds pause]

And your new look gives you renewed confidence and control. You can see that your clothes are getting loose. You have shed so much of your extra weight. You go out and meet people and everyone is just awed by your transformation. Your friends and colleagues just can't stop complementing you. People are now coming to you for tips on losing weight. You have this charisma and confidence when you are in public.

[5 seconds pause]

You are drinking the right amount of water; keeping your body hydrated and healthy. Your mind is sharper, clearer and more focused. You are sleeping better and deeper at night. You are waking feeling refreshed and full of energy and enthusiasm in the morning. You are more flexible and confident in your body. You are more content with what you have. You work with full passion. You have increased your productivity and efficiency.

[5 seconds pause]

And now you are at your perfect body – you ideal weight and size. And you continue to exercise and maintain that level of fitness and stamina. You never knew you could enjoy your work out sessions so much and grow so rapidly. You are not just physically fit but mentally you are at your best level. You feel emotionally balanced and mentally strong. You know you can face any challenge and climb any mountain. You now have full control over your life.

[5 seconds pause]

You are always in control. You can just drift down now, drift down and into sleep. And while you are in a world of your dreams, the universe is working for you. All your wishes will manifest in time. But for that you need to rest now. So sleep, sleep, sleep. You feel so relaxed. Saying this, she sprinkles droplets of magical water from her wand. And the Sleep Fairy fades away in her golden coloured ball of light. Your room is now filled with the aroma of the magical water that is lulling you to sleep.

You are almost asleep and can no longer make sense of your thoughts. You are already in that state of deep sleep. Everything is relaxed. Your mind is calm. Your body is completely relaxed. You are entering a deep, deep, level of relaxed sleep.

Your mind can wonder and to dreams. Your body relaxing as you drift deeper now; deeper down into sleep.

12. Weight Loss Hypnosis (Before Sleep) – II (60 minutes)

For this hypnosis, I want you to lie down comfortably on your bed or sofa. You can adjust your pillows and blankets. You may fall asleep while listening to this audio or just after that. This hypnosis should best be enjoyed using headphones.

Listen to my voice with full focus and follow my instructions. If your mind wanders during the course of the hypnosis, gently bring it back. It is the very nature of the mind to find ways to escape attention. Do not worry; this hypnosis isn't for your conscious mind. Through this hypnosis, I will be commanding your subconscious mind. Your subconscious mind is always awake and active even when the conscious mind is asleep. So, the hypnosis will work and your subconscious mind will find ways to get you the desired weight loss results that you seek. For that, you need to simply relax. Let go of any doubts and fears. Everything is going to be alright. This hypnosis will go perfectly fine. Right now, you need to simply relax and let go of any thoughts. Loosen up your body. First I will be relaxing your physical body to make it easier for your subconscious mind to follow my instructions and act on it. The physical body relaxation will calm down your mind as well. The calmer you are the more attentive your subconscious mind is. So, all in all, you don't need to do anything at all. You simply stay relaxed. So, let's begin.

I will count backwards from five to one and when I reach one, you are going to allow your eyelids to shut down and relax.

Five: You loosen up your body a little. You adjust your shoulders, relax your jaw, and release all the stress from your body.

Four: You feel sleepy and drowsy as you stare at the ceiling. You feel so sleepy and drowsy.

Three: Your eyelids are becoming heavy, so heavy. You are finding it difficult to keep them open.

Two: The hypnosis is taking over your mind. You feel the sleep entering your eyes, making you want to close them

One: And you shut your eyelids. Relaxing and calming down in this peaceful state. Going within, deep within.

[30 seconds pause]

Listen to my voice and follow my instructions. You can now feel a sense of calm and relaxation all over your body. And while a part of your mind will follow my instructions, another part of you will keep a gentle focus on the flow of your breathing. Nice and steady breaths – the in-breath and the out-breath.

[5 seconds pause]

When I name a body part, you will feel that part and at the same time create an image of that part in your mind.

[5 seconds pause]

Toes, fingers, hands, feet, shins, calves, thighs, buttocks tensing up all the muscles in your body. All the way up to the back of the neck, the head and the face. And take a long inhale breath and as you exhale relax the whole body. Let everything go. It's really grateful preparing the body for sleep and also meditation. Just try that once more, just tensing up the whole body from the tips of the toes to all the way up. Imagine like a maximum wave of energy just tensing up the head.

[5 seconds pause]

Once more let begin to tension the body from the toes, up to the legs, to the arm, all the way to the top of the head. This body relaxation practice is a very important part of this hypnosis as it is taking you into deeper and deeper levels of the hypnotic trance. The more your body relaxes, the more ably your subconscious mind receives my command and charts out different ways to act on them. So, continuing with this relaxation now. Now, tightening all the belly muscles, all the way up to front of the body and take a deep breath. Even the face is crunched up as you inhale, and then exhale and really let go. Let go of anything that you are willing to release.

[5 seconds pause]

Allow yourself some time to relax and come into the present time and really notice the sense of hearing. May be there is some random sound that are outside or inside the room, or outside the building. Just allow yourself to hear, everything you hear.

[5 seconds pause]

Let yourself be aware now of the sense of the touch of the body whether cousins or pillows or wherever you are lying, whatever your hands and feet are touching. Have sense of where your body is actually being supported. Touch of the skin against the cloths you are wearing.

[5 seconds pause]

Closing the eyes and noticing the black space when you close the eyes. That space between the eyebrows where we look into the infinite space. Just noticing, noticing the sense of taste you have when you feel the tongue in your mouth.

[5 seconds pause]

Through the breath may be a sense of smell, it may be a familiar smell of the room around you. May be you are sensing a smell of a perfume or a something you are wearing or just the smell of your cloths.

[5 seconds pause]

Bring yourself into the present moment. Becoming aware with the breath in the very simple moment of the breath into the nose and out through the nose. Just become aware of the breath, its sound, the taste, the smell, the touch of the body. Gather you into this present moment. Pause for a moment, relax. Just feel the breath flow as the wind in the valleys, and the hills of the Mother Nature. Feel the breath moving inside and the outside the body as they are moving between the trees, through the earth of the Mother Nature herself.

[5 seconds pause]

Noticing where the breath touches as it comes through the nose and out through the nose. Breathe moving freely and nicely as its find its own passage of coming and going. Letting every beneath the breath simply being aware by breathing. Pause for a moment, relax. Acknowledge the simple movement of the breath.

[5 seconds pause]

With awareness I am practicing meditation with this form of awareness with this safe vessel on which I am resting. Really connect to that breath. Visualize the blood in the blood stream, the water in the body like the rivers and the flowing nature of the water in the rivers through mountains and valleys of the Mother Nature herself. Pause for a moment, relax. Have that sense of connection as you breathe the flow of your blood or the flow of the water in your body. The water that has been held in your cells so the water absorb into the landscape. Pause for a moment, relax. Really feeling yourself as the Mother Nature has herself. The rise and fall of your body, the curve and the turn in your body, little raises and little valleys may be between the toes and in the fingers, and the flow of the breath, the flow of the water and blood in the body. So will be landscape, you will be your own landscape of the Mother Nature.

[5 seconds pause]

Just feeling flow, visualizing flow through the whole body. Bring pure awareness now to the body as we move round in a rotation of the consciousness. Pause for a moment, relax. Now, I want you to visualize your body as the tree, the great majestic tree with your feet connected to mother earth. Feel the upper extremities of your body moving up through the tree trunk to the brown shoes in the leaves on the trees. Either with pure awareness or maybe you visualize awareness manifesting as little flock of birds that will be landing in your tree.

[5 seconds pause]

Become aware of a little bird of awareness of the tip of your nose and the left eye and the right eye. And top lip and the bottom lip. A little bird of awareness arrives in your chin and the tip of the left ear and the right ear to the top of the head and the back of the head. Pause for a moment, relax. The curve of the back of your neck, the little bird of awareness is taking your full attention to back of your neck, the notch of the neck and the front of the throat. Pause for a moment, relax. A little bird of the awareness is landing on your right collar bone. Tip of the right shoulder and the right shoulder blade and the right arm pit and the top of the right arm, and the inner elbow and the elbow, the forearm and the wrist.

[5 seconds pause]

The little bird of awareness landing in the palm of your right hand, and the tip of the right thumb, index finger, middle finger, ring finger and little finger, a little bird of awareness landing on the back of your right hand. This body relaxation practice is a very important part of this hypnosis as it is taking you into deeper and deeper levels of the hypnotic trance. The more your body relaxes, the more ably your subconscious mind receives my command and charts out different ways to act on them. So, continuing with this relaxation now.

[5 seconds pause]

The left color bone and the left shoulder and the left shoulder blade and the left arm pit and the top of the left arm, a little bird of the awareness is arriving the inner elbow, forearm and wrist and the little bird of awareness is arriving the thumb of your left hand, left thumb, your left index finger, middle finger, ring finger and little finger. Pause for a moment, relax. The little bird of the awareness is just arriving at the back of your left hand. And the front of your chest, the lower ribs at the left side and right side. . The more your body relaxes, the more ably your subconscious mind receives my command and charts out different ways to act on them. Little bird of awareness is landing on your belly button, left hip and the right hip, then the each vertebras of the spine to the very top of the spine.

[5 seconds pause]

The left side of the body and the right side of the body, the left buttock the little bird of awareness are touching becoming aware of the left thigh and the back of the thigh and the back of the knee, and the shins, the calf's, ankles and tip of the left heel and the sole of the left foot. Pause for a moment, relax. The toes, tip of the left toe, second toe, third toe, fourth toe and a little bird of awareness touching a little toe. This body relaxation practice is a very important part of this hypnosis as it is taking you into deeper and deeper levels of the hypnotic trance. The more your body relaxes, the more ably your subconscious mind receives my command and charts out different ways to act on them. So, continuing with this relaxation now.

[5 seconds pause]

Bring your awareness to the right buttock, the right thigh, the thigh, the back of the knee, the right knee, the shin and the calf, the ankle and the heel. The more your body relaxes, the more ably your subconscious mind receives my command and charts out different ways to act on them. The bird of awareness is touching the sole of the right foot. The top of the foot, right big toe, second toe, third toe, fourth toe and a little bird of awareness touching a little toe.

[5 seconds pause]

Now see your body as a majestic tree grounded to your feet in mother earth. Simple bird of awareness now all is showing the awareness in the whole body. Feeling each little bird placed on the left leg and right leg, whole of the body, the left arm and the right arm and the whole of your head. Pause for a moment, relax. Feel that each little bird brings pure awareness to the majestic tree that is your body alive, wildish nature of the body, alive in every cell. Pause for a moment, relax. Feel your vital life force like light of energy through your body, through into mother earth and then into mother earth through into your body. Feel that vital nature that life force power.

[5 seconds pause]

You feel completely aligned and connected – connected to nature, connected to your soul, connected to your highest self. Pause for a moment, relax. You are safe. You are here in this present moment. You are safe.

[30 seconds pause]

Now I want you to imagine yourself to be sitting on a beach, relaxing.

It's a beautiful sunny day out you can hear the sound of the waves crashing on the shore. You can smell the sand and the ocean. The warmth of the rays of the sun feels so pleasant on your body. You can feel as if it is making your face glow. Your face muscles relax. And you can feel the warmth trickle down on to your neck. Now, you can feel it on your shoulders. And your shoulders relax, dropping down, releasing any tension they may have been holding onto. Your arms, relax. Feel the warmth going into your hands and fingers, relaxing them completely.

[5 seconds pause]

And you now feel it on your chest – that relaxing warmth of the Sun. you breathe in, feeling relaxed, breathe out releasing any tension you may be holding onto. And again breathe in, feeling relaxed, breathe out releasing any tension you may be holding onto. Breathe in, feeling relaxed, breathe out releasing tensions.

[5 seconds pause]

You can now feel the pleasant warmth going down to your tummy, relaxing it. Easy and relaxed, the feeling is so pleasant. Feel that relaxation moving down into your buttocks. Now that warmth moves into your thighs. Feel relaxed.

[5 seconds pause]

Now feel the warmth and relaxation spreading into the legs, relaxing them fully. And now feel the warmth in your feet, the soles of your feet, and your toes – all your toes feeling relaxed.

[5 seconds pause]

Feel your entire body being relaxed and comfortable.

[20 seconds pause]

You must be feeling so relaxed right now. You have never felt so calm ever before. What you are experiencing right now is that state of hypnosis when you are made to relax through commands and within the guided visualization you are taken into a deeper level of trance. You are in that trance right now. Now, whatever I say, your subconscious mind will get it in its clearest form and meaning.

[5 seconds pause]

You are the creator of your life. Stay aware about what you think and say because the universe is listening to your thoughts and intentions. You never know on which thought the universe may begin to work. This is especially true when you sit to meditate or are in a deep state of subliminal awareness as you are now. Whatever you conceive now in your mind will fructify into the real world.

[5 seconds pause]

Your subconscious mind knows what needs to be done to lose the excess weight. It knows that you have to eat healthy and nutritious food. It knows that ones you make it a habit to consume only nutritious food, your body will respond immediately. You need to take care of your body just like this body takes care of you. Your body is the tool with which you experience this gift of life. From now on, you will feed your body with healthy food. You will stay away from all that is unhealthy and harmful for your health. You will automatically turn away these unhealthy food items. Your mind and body are now aligning with each other for your higher good. From now on, your mind will think about only what is good for your body. Your mind will not create cravings that may harm your body.

[5 seconds pause]

From now on, health is your priority. Every meal you have, every bite you eat is precious. From now on, you will eat your meals with full awareness. You will eat each bite mindfully, chewing it for at least twenty times. And you eat slowly, enjoying the flavors and the textures of the food. You enjoy your meals so much more than you ever did before.

[5 seconds pause]

And now you look forward to your exercise sessions. You have found ways to move and keep your physical body active. It can be through any means of your choice – from jogging, to running, to cycling, to playing your favorite sport. You sweat it out in the field so that you can attain and maintain your ideal body weight and size.

[5 seconds pause]

And in this state of trance, whatever your mind can conceive of an ideal body, it can surely achieve it. That's why I want you to imagine in your mind how would your ideal self look like. And this state of deep trance, know that whatever you create will surely turn into your reality. So, take your time and visualize yourself in your perfect state of health and wellbeing. Feel the feeling. See from the eyes of the perfect-looking you. Feel the confidence and charisma that comes with this perfect body and fitness.

[5 seconds pause]

See your perfect self as clearly and as vividly as possible. The more deeply you feel yourself having attained that ideal weight and size the better.

[5 seconds pause]

Become that perfect you; have the feeling of health and wellbeing resonate deep within you, and staying in that zone for a while.

[10 minutes pause]

You are already so peaceful. If you are not asleep, you are about to enter the state of a deep peaceful sleep all by itself. You can feel a sense of deep relaxation covering your entire body right from the tip of your toes to the crown of your head. As if you are resting and relaxing in an envelope of peace. Every cell and every muscle in your body is relaxed. You feel so light. As if there is no body. You are light as a feather,

[5 seconds pause]

You feel so light, so relaxed; just ready to fall asleep. To help you sleep faster, let's count backwards from 100. So let's relax the mind by really slowly counting down from 100. 99... 98... 97... 96... 95... continue counting. Each number makes you feel comfortable and relaxed. If you lose count that's fine, just pick up from wherever you remember you lost count.

[The narrator must speak the numbers in fading voice]

95... 94... 93... 92... 91... 90... 89... 88

That's right. You are doing fine. Continue counting backwards. And if you lose count, just start again from where you left.

Feel that your breath as your companion; breathing in a sense of calmness and peace and breathing out, just letting go. Allowing your breath to soothe and nourish you.

[10 seconds pause]

Your breath becomes slower, deeper.

Allow the breath to lower you deeper and deeper into sleep.

[10 seconds pause]

 It's okay to rest.

[10 seconds pause]

You are held. You are safe. No worries. Simply rest and relax.

[10 seconds pause]

Relaxing deeper and deeper.

[30 seconds pause]

You are calm and relaxed. You are as relaxed as one can be. There's nothing more that you can do. There's nothing else that can be done. You are free. You are relaxed. You are ready to drift into deep, deep sleep.

www.ingramcontent.com/pod-product-compliance
Lightning Source LLC
Chambersburg PA
CBHW080632170426
43209CB00008B/1555